Neither Lost nor Stolen

but

Straid

(Ballyclare)

by Ernest McAlister Scott

*Published by Shanway Press,
Belfast*

*Far have you wandered overseas of longing
And now you drowse, and now you well may weep
When all the recollections come a-thronging
Of this rude country where your fathers sleep.*

Neil Munro, 'To exiles'

*Remember the days of old
Consider the years of many generations
Ask thy father and he will show you
Thine elders and they will tell you.*

Deuteronomy Ch.32v.7

Dedication

This second book on local village history is once again
dedicated to my long suffering wife Marjory
and my four daughters and their families.

When the muse was upon me when writing
they could not get me to talk
but in periods of no ideas
they could not get me to shut up.

Acknowledgements

As every author realises no book would ever be published without the help of a number of people whose expertise is essential to the production. This is very evident to the writer of this volume and he gladly acknowledges same.

To that virtuoso of the artist's brush, Janette McKendry, I have not enough praise to adequately express for her brilliant painting of old Straid on the front cover, which takes me back many years.

To Maureen Robinson of Islandmagee, whose expertise with a computer leaves me aghast, I owe a great deal inasmuch she had to decipher my handwriting, type the manuscript and proof read the finished work.

To all who lent photographs to me I am grateful and I owe a lot to MichaelMcKernon of Shanway Press for his expertise in typesetting and lay out of book pages.

In conclusion I would very much like to express my appreciation to Newtownabbey Borough Council and in particular to Ms. Samantha Curry for her unstinting help in the production of this book.

Introduction

I have stated elsewhere in this book how privileged I have been during my lifetime to have been born in an era which had been unchanged for two hundred years and was just beginning to see the horizons opening up with the invention of the internal combustion engine and in my youth the growth of traffic starting with Henry Ford's famous Models A and T, the famous "tin lizzies".

From the time of the horse and cart to the landing of man on the moon, spacecraft going to Mars and other planets it is indeed a tribute to man's ingenuity and whether man evolved, as most of us believe, in the image of God the Father, or as others would have us believe that he took his first faltering steps in the Great Rift Valley in East Africa it really does not detract from his achievements.

However, there are a number of flies in the ointment. The invention of television has completely ruined conversation; the computer has ruined handwriting and the writing of letters. The fax and mobile phone through texting has ruined English spelling and the calculator has fossilized our brain.

Man regrettably now has not the time for good conversation nor dare he, as we did long ago, have our doors open so that any neighbour could drop in when they pleased.

These are the drawbacks to progress but my hope is that Straid, through becoming a dormitory town, may keep its peace and tranquillity as it has done in the past and continue to rate high amongst those places where one could have peace and happiness.

Archie Reid

Tribute

It is with heavy heart I write about Straid following my history "BALLYNURE DURING THE LAST FOUR HUNDRED YEARS".

The reason for this being, that having succeeded in getting it ready and published my late lamented mentor Archie Reid promised to write a book on Ballyclare and its satellite villages, Ballyeaston, Doagh taking in Burnside and made me promise to bring out one about Straid, thus completing his aim to leave for future generations the legacy of all the villages lying to the North East of the Six Mile Water Valley.

The love of the late Archie's life, after Lindy, was the valley in which he was born and where he left a legacy, never equalled before, of films and documentary writings. It is in Archie's memory I lay this book before you, especially as Archie before he died completed his book entitled "BALLYCLARE, 4000 YEARS BENEATH THE HOLESTONE", I therefore dedicate it in his memory and hope it will persuade readers to find out for themselves the massive contribution Archie made to local history in the Six Mile Water Valley.

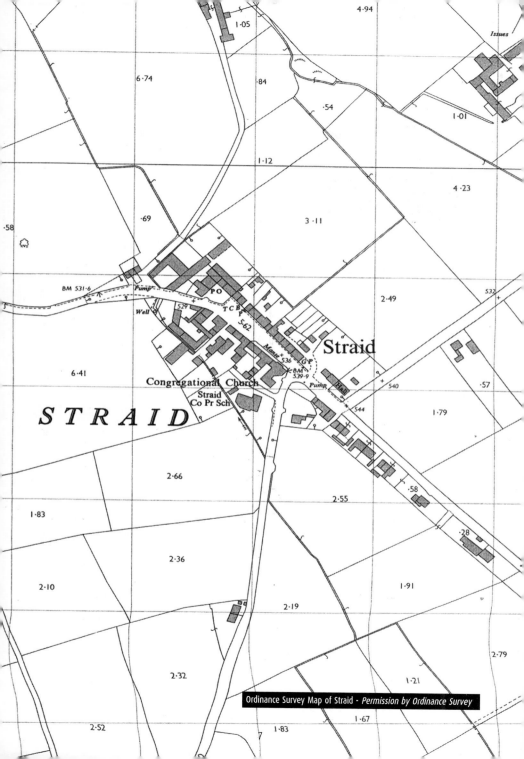

Ordinance Survey Map of Straid · *Permission by Ordinance Survey*

Skinner's Road Map of Straid showing estates. Circa 1777.

Above: View from Straid hinterland from Straid Hill.

Below: View of Old Straid village painted by Jeanette McHendry

Straid inhanitants 1907. (l - R) - Back Row: Sam Millar, M. J. Johnston, M. Simms, M. Millar, C. Boyd & J. Millar
Second Row: Mrs Johnston, Mary Ellen Johnston, S. PArk, L. Boyd, H. Park, C. McMurtry, Cissy Johnston & Jane Johnston
Third Row: Mrs Blackadder, Bell Howie, Mary Greer, Mrs Martha Park & J. Park
Fourth Row: T. Wilson (The Mill), H. Millar, R. G. Longmore, Maggie Simms, Martha Park & J. Park Junior.
A. Johnston collection.

Straid

In writing about Straid the local historian is confronted with a number of problems right away, the main one being "What was there before the Village?" Not a lot of work by historians has been done, certainly not by local historians, about life in Ireland before the Anglo-Norman invasion and up to and before the reign of Elizabeth the First.

The Celtic race flourished as an identifiable culture beginning around 7000 B.C. in Europe, principally the Czech Republic and Hungary. Their influences reached England around the 6th century B.C.and was characterized by techniques of iron- working, resulting in improved weapons and agricultural implements.

Between the first and third century B.C. they came to Ireland where they settled and flourished. From 43-85 AD the Romans invaded Britain, which remained occupied for 360 years but, as the Celtic nature of the Britons was displaced, it flourished in Ireland where the Romans never conquered.

While one may be left wondering what this has to do with Straid it will be seen that this part of the world was linked to these people up to about the fifteen hundreds.

These Celts had in Ireland their own laws, called the Brehon Laws that governed all and was the indigenous law of both Ireland and Scotland before the conquest.

Later on it will be seen how it affected Straid, but to do so it is necessary to understand what the Brehon law entailed.

It is named after the primary practitioners of the law in Ireland who were akin to Judges or Jurists, but in practice more akin to a mediator.

Brehons continued the Druidic tradition after the Druids fell from grace. Imagine a legal system that respected individuals first and property second, a system that revered the sanctity of the contract and wherein the environment was of paramount importance; women had equal property rights to men and could divorce. One owed a duty of hospitality and protection to strangers.

Imagine also a legal system of self-help that needed no court or police force to enforce it, since all its citizens respected it.

These were some of the principles and attributes of Brehon law existing in Ireland from the Celtic settlement, before Christ, up until the seventeenth century and the reign of Elizabeth I.

One of these ancient Brehon laws required that there should be at any crossing ford over a river a signal light for the guidance of travellers and there were certain officials appointed whose duty it was to take charge of them.

Up past the Masonic Hall on the Seskin Road going towards Carrickfergus at a bad bend on the road at the bottom of the first hill on land belonging to Mr Dennis Boyd there is a small stream bridged. I would defy any person to imagine a swirling torrent of a river at this place but knowing that, before the new Scots settlers drained the land most of the rivers we know now were much wider and swampy and would therefore be a more hazardous crossing.

*In Brehon law times this crossing was called Aghasolas (pronounced A-solia) a ford of light. This ford is marked today on the Ordinance Survey Maps as Fool Ford and is still known as such by the older inhabitants. This is one of the more glaring mistakes of the Royal Engineers in doing the Ordinance Surveys of the eighteen forties where they try to Anglo-size Irish words. Some officer who knew a little of the Irish language must have thought that the latter part of the word Salach, dirty or foul, and hence we get the name "fool ford".

*See "The Diocese of Down & Conner. Rev. James Lavery Vol.III Page 176.

Thus we get an inkling of the age of the land surrounding Straid from Caldhame to the Commons of Carrick to the Quarterlands and Four Score Acres. It is hard for us now a days to imagine our forefathers in those early days having to cope with wild animals such as the wolf as the last Irish wolf was killed at Wolfhill above Belfast in 1718.

The area of land around Straid was unique as, along with Coleraine which was also under the influence of the Anglo-Normans, Carrickfergus was known as the County and Town of Carrickfergus as was Coleraine.

Queen Elizabeth I established these boundaries under her great seal dated 10th day of June 1601 in the forty-third year of her reign.

This took in an area roughly running from Kilroot to Raloo through to but not including Ballynure and on to the Flush at Bruslee and then on through Carntall to Silverstream at Greenisland. These borders had to be ridden every seven years by the Mayor of Carrickfergus who had to detour to partake of a stirrup cup in the garden of the Mansion House in Straid owned by Henry Ellis. Presumably this was to prove to Ellis who was a Burgess and High Sheriff of Carrickfergus that he was doing his duty.

This was called the Riding of the Boundaries and is equal to the West and East Ridings of Yorkshire to consolidate the area.

Thus we see today that Straid played a very important part in the Town and County as the town lands that we know, namely Little Ballymena, Straidlands, Lisglass, were included in these Boundaries.

Potato digging - circa 1940. (For comparison see page 84)

The following is a poem written by the author and Presented at a seminar in Loughry Agricultural College

Seventy Years Ago

The ring of steel-shod hooves is heard along the lonely road
In winter's dusk, man and horse, each makes for his abode
But master yet has work to do, his charges he must feed
The plough tomorrow must be pulled it is the urgent need
In breeches warm and leggings tight a warm bran mash he makes
With contented puffs at plug-filled pipe sweet smelling straw he shakes
Not yet for him the cosy fire, horse and cow come always first
Or maybe yet a sickly sow, or a calf which must be nursed.

Seedtimes age-old miracle is here, Scotch oats the sower wisely buys
The corn fiddle's happy song the lark drowns out in clear blue April skies
The ploughing's done and winter's frosts left seed beds in good sheer.
The potato pits have gone, the hedges trimmed and sheughs are running clear.
In May the creaking cart winds right o'er the head rig bare
And patient horse shall stop and start in drills like arrows there
Placed in dung, the sprouted spud life's cycle bravely starts
A ten-fold yield with loving care, the prayer in country hearts.

With swishing tails the clegs to beat the horses bravely plod
The reaper's song drowns out the corncrakes screech o'er stubbles sod
A blazing June, a Constable scene, the hay-ricks sprout a space
No panic here, with fork and rake, man's toil is blessed with grace.
The grass-seed hay is saved, potatoes hoed and turnips growing fast
The ewes are shorn, the wool is sold, and flies o'er trout are cast
Copper sulphate and the soda-ash over potato haulm is sprayed
In Ireland memories slowly die as when the hungry years dismayed

The August days go slowly past the meadow hay is saved
The valley's filled with golden grain with each breeze the ears are waved
In each sheltered farmyard, thatched and roped. The pikes of hay abound
An expectant hush is felt; once again the harvest is almost round
The binder's out! The sheaves fall fast; the stooks in rows are set
And as at dusk, when looking round, the farmer nods, and yet
He feels a Higher Presence there; his faith to him is dear
Seedtime and harvest shall not cease this is the promise clear.

In each haggard, row on row, the corn stacks against the sky
Stand out like Zulu kraals as the hunters pass them by
October frosts are light as yet but the grain is safe and snug
And a bigger task appears when the spuds have to be dug
A fortnight off from school and a shilling for each day
Each mother anxious waits at the weekend for the pay
New trousers to be bought and the old ones handed down
To be rich nigh seventy years ago was no more than half-a-crown.

For man and master in those days each contented with their lot
Toiled long and hard, money in hand before a single item bought
At Harvest Home in lusty voice, their Maker's praise sing out
Their heartfelt thanks for another year with no room for any doubt
Ill fares the land when men like these will eventually pass away
And I in the Hallowed Acre kneel and feel guided there to pray
That I may yet become like these, before I cross the Bar
And maybe reach the Golden Shore, if Jehovah thinks it's not too far.

A Ferguson-
own driving a
Marshall Mill
circa 1940.

Agriculture

It is perhaps fitting that I should begin to write about Straid in the context of agriculture inasmuch, except for a period of industry in the bauxite mines on Straid Hill, agriculture has been the main stay of its prosperity.

"Where farming goes other arts follow, farmers therefore are the foundation of civilisation". So says the proverb and no individual or organisation can exist without feeding the inner man, or to be correct these days, person.

No words of mine could convey to anyone under the age of sixty the absolute tranquillity of the countryside before a certain Mr Henry Ford and a Mr Harry Ferguson came on the scene, more of both later.

Now-a-days when one looks round the countryside in June and July all one sees are fields completely shorn of grass and left bare with all in the silo pit. Seventy years ago the only noise during the busy day was the rattle of a horse reaper and the stamp of the horse's hoof to shift the horseflies (clegs). No other noise was heard, as the making of hay was all manual work and heavy dusty work at that.

Two examples of 'cut-down lorries' used as tractors.

The typical farmer's day in that period would have started after breakfast at around six o'clock when he harnessed two horses to go to reap grass for hay in the hope that the ubiquitous clegs would not have surfaced and leaving the cut grass to lie and cure in the sun then enter the potato field to use the grubber to remove the sides of the drills for the drill plough to make them up again to put fresh soil among the roots. After lunch, which probably consisted of British Queen potatoes in July, home grown scallions and fresh buttermilk, the hay that was ready to be put into cocks or ricks, as they were known, (rucks in Ulster Scots). All this work in those far off days was leisurely, as the sunshine could be trusted to last for weeks on end. All this labour was worthy of a work by Constable. Just before the end of the day the potato field was again entered and the grubbed drills were then set up again with a drill plough, the reasons for this being potato leaves close up tight at dusk and therefore will not be covered with soil.

It must be remembered that at this particular time the horse held sway and was the most important animal on the farm but the horses' days were numbered as various farmers were beginning to think of mechanization now that the motor lorry was taking the place of the horse and cart in taking produce from the Straid area to Belfast.

A local farmer in 1935, one Jim Boyd, whose farm stead stood where Ellisland Mews now are, decided to get something mechanical to bring the produce from his out-lying fields on the Caldhame and Ballynure Roads and cut down on the slow moving horse. He tasked a garage owner in Ballyclare, Samuel Girvan who was an expert in improvisation, to cut the chassis of an old Morris Commercial lorry in half, refit the rear wheels at the rear of the cut chassis and fit an extra gear-box on the drive shaft, giving the amazing result that if both gear boxes were in first gear the machine reversed and if in reverse gear it went forward. Wedges were then cut out of two oversized tyres and fitted over the rear wheels and the author remembers watching as eight strong men and it having a tug-of-war with the men losing.

It must be remembered that in those far off days petrol was delivered to one's door at one and sixpence ($7^1/_2$p) per gallons in a Pratt's tin. When a local farmer saw this converted tractor as they were called he scathingly dubbed it immediately a "mechanical abortion".

Just afterwards in 1936 Harry Ferguson and Aston Martin produced the Ferguson-Brown tractor with a hydraulic lift for implements but with the drawback of having to be either going forward or backwards before the hydraulic lift would work. However in 1938, Harry Ferguson and Henry Ford produced the Ford-Ferguson tractor, one of the best little tractors ever produced and forerunner of the famous TE20 Ferguson.

In 1939 at the out-break of World War Two these Ford-Ferguson tractors were in optimum demand for food production but were strictly rationed to the farmers who had the most arable land. They were produced originally to run on petrol but at the outbreak of hostilities a vaporiser was fitted allowing them to run on refined paraffin.

1938 Ford Ferguson.

The other tractor in great demand was the famous Fordson model N and various other makes were purchased. This was the end of the old way of farming which had lasted for generations and heralded the way of agriculture as we see it today with the demise of an awful lot of wildlife, which some young people have never seen.

I might say that at my age I have been very privileged to have spent my youth among wildlife the young no longer see. How often now-a-days would anyone see a hare behaving as if she had broken a leg and limping away to distract your attention from her young leveret in a tuft of grass.

How many large flocks of plover (peesweeps) do we see or be stung with a horse fly (cleg) a member of the family of dipterans whose female members suck blood from animals and humans.

Years ago, on a beautiful summer's day, on a walk in the countryside, one could hear little save the chirping of grasshoppers, see myriads of dragon flies over head and to cap it all, the beautiful song of the lark in the clear air above all. It is perhaps a very sobering thought to those of my generation who embraced the invention of pesticides after World War II and used them with abandon to find we have forever denuded the hedgerows and road verges of wildlife with D.D.T.

We have, I greatly fear, in our lifetime destroyed the environment to an extent that there is no turning back, and never again will I be able to be apoplectic with rage at not being able to get to sleep owing to the raucous racket of the corncrake unless I go to Fermanagh and the far west of Ireland. So much for progress.

As a senior citizen fast approaching octogenarian status one other thing amazes me. Pre the 1950's the average size of the Ulster farms was 35 acres and in those days the farm usually supported an average of eight cows, either one or two horses, young stock for replacements, a couple of sows and a number of other pigs for fattening. The lady of the house was responsible for all the poultry, the returns of which bought all the food needed for the house, apart from vegetables, which were home grown. Now-a-days the average farm is 98 acres and to illustrate the changes in agriculture I can say that north of Straid on the Sheskin Road, three herds of cows, over 100 head each, are situated and one has to pass through the town lands of Straid, Dairylands, Bryantang, Dunturkey, Legaloy, Toberdowney and Skilganaban before another herd of one hundred plus is encountered in Ballynure. What has now taken the cows place?

At first glance the absence of cows in these areas would leave one to believe that cow numbers would be greatly reduced but in perusing the Department of Agriculture and Rural Development's census we find that in June 1981 the number of cows totalled 270,459, i.e. cows either in milk or in calf while the latest figures we have in 2005 for cows in calf or in milk is 290,530.
How come a rise of 20,071 cows in calf or milk from 1981 to 2005, 24 years only, and how is it done with 30,955 farmers (full time) in 1981 falling to 18,159 full time farmers in 2005?

All figures attributed to D.A.R.D.Census.

This to my mind is the farms becoming larger and an increase of 20,000 milk cows is undoubtedly due to specialization, greater mechanization and improved work methods requiring less labour.

To answer my question, what has taken the place of cows in the farms which have none? Once again from 1960 when cow numbers have trebled beef cow numbers have also trebled and this together with their suckler calves will have utilised the remaining land.

The fact that the number of full time farmers has almost halved over the past 35 years is undoubtedly due to poor returns from farming and the need for off farm income, increased mechanization, efficiency in the use of the farmers' time and also the lack of availability of additional land for purchase to enable expansion.

In my introduction in this book about Straid, I mentioned the Celts in Ireland appearing between the first and third century B.C. but long before that was the Stone Age to earliest man roughly nine thousand years ago. Due to the dry conditions of the soil and the presence of flint it is nearly certain that the dry lands around Straid were most certainly farmed by hunter-gatherers. A hoard of flint arrowheads found in Riverdale, Ballyclare in 1968 has been dated to four thousand years ago. Anyone can take a walk from Straid down the Caldhame Road and view the right hand side and find that over two thousand years ago a fort was built with an outside ditch to be seen to this day and is known as Wiley's fort. Another fort which was levelled in the 19th century was in the town land of Bryantang overlooking Straid Dam and had a commanding view over the country to Wiley's fort. The field where it stood is known to this day as the Forth Field.

Just discovered in 2005 in the town land of Castletown, Ballynure was another ringed fort of immense proportions, which was in visible distance of another fort in Ballylagan.

In a time of danger, either beacon fires would be lit at the summit or a runner sent from one to the other with a warning.

Therefore agriculture has been the mainstay of the Straid area for the past 4000 years and looking round the well tilled fields and neat hedges and farmsteads of today one is nearly sure that Straid's agricultural prosperity will be in safe in the hands of today's farmers.

Before leaving the chapter on agriculture it would be an advantage to future generations who may want to know something about the old system of measuring land now that the European hectare holds sway.

It is not generally known that five and a half yards, which is a perch, pole or rod, is the distance a man can broadcast seed from an apron on each side as he walks, the word pole coming from the fact that when the sower would reach the field hedge he would step 5½ yards and plant a pole to aim for on his return journey. A furlong comprising of slightly over 40 perches, being 1/8 of a mile, was considered the distance two horses could plough when ploughing furrows each facing other, known as gathering and going the same distance over the field and bringing each part together resulting in a hint.

This was called statute, or English measure, but to complicate the issue two other units of measurement were sometimes used. Irish measure has seven yards to the perch, making eight furlongs to the mile measure 2240 yards against 1760 yards for an English mile, giving the proverb
"A smile is like an Irish mile, it goes a long way".

An English acre was 440 sq. yards against 480 in Irish measure.

Cunningham or Plantation measure was a method of ground measurement used by the Scottish planters which was much larger than either statute or Irish measure resulting in these settlers obtaining much more land.

In finishing writing about agriculture a quotation comes to mind, which shows mankind has changed.

The quotation written in 1756 by Oliver Goldsmith
warns of material expansion in the type of world we have today:-

"Ill fares the land, to hastening ills a prey

Where wealth accumulates and men decay.

Princes and Lords may flourish or may fade

A breath can take them, as a breath has made

But a bold peasantry, their countries pride

When once destroy'd can never be supplied

For him light labour spread her wholesome store

Just gave what life requir'd, but gave no more

His best companions, ignorance and health

His best riches, ignorance and wealth."

Agriculture has come a long way since 1756!

The Straid Smithy - now long gone.

Blacksmith

There is no doubt that the two most important artisans in a rural area were the Blacksmith and the Carpenter.

Before the industrial revolution from the middle 1700's to the middle of 1800's all hand tools and kitchen utensils and even harning irons to set beside the fire to harden oat cake and items such as tongs and pokers were handmade by the Blacksmith along with all the iron needed by the Carpenter.

When we remember that the Carpenter had to provide all the hand crafted implements for the farm, such as carts, harrows and most importantly hand crafting such items as churns driven by horse power and hand churns known as plunge churns because of the action by hands up and down of the paddle for churning.

All irons on carts, harrow tines and farm gates were fashioned in iron and one thinks of the work in drilling holes to rivet a gate with a breast-barrel and bit at the time when there was no electrical power, the Blacksmith had to work more than eight hours in a day and further back in time by candlelight.

Thus we see in the 1860 s, 147 years ago, in the Griffith rateable valuation for the Larne Rural District there was a Blacksmith in Straid called Wm. Bell but in 1901 census the Blacksmith was a James McCann, whose wife Mary and sons James and Samuel were listed as Blacksmith helpers and having a brother John and a sister Jeannie at school.

The author can remember the McCann brothers very well and many a job was done for him in the old smithy with the hand bellows blowing sparks up the wide chimney and he can still smell the horses burning hoof where the red hot shoe was making its pattern to fit the shoe comfortably on the hoof.

In the Larne Times of the month of July 1957 we can read an account of Straid s Twin men of Iron closing down the family business of blacksmithing and pointing out for the first time, the village, in over a 100 years, has no Blacksmith.

'Twin men of Iron'

The McCann twins, James and Samuel

The Blacksmith in those days pre 1957 acted sometimes more as a farrier than a Blacksmith. Certainly if only one man ran a forge he would be interrupted many times daily to shoe horses and McCann Bros. were no exception, save that in the last 15 years of their working life they acted very ungraciously towards the clients that rather than run the gauntlet of their truculence, farmers went to Barr's of Ballynure where three blacksmiths would shoe horses at the one smithy.

Now, McCann's were artisans rather than farriers and their work was more intricate and the more difficult the better. Either man could lay a scythe blade to the handle so that the reach in mowing suited the worker and they were expert in tempering red-hot steel in oil.

This is not meant in any way to belittle the farrier as pre 1947 and the advent of the famous TE20 tractor, the famous grey Fergie the horse was the main means of traction and indeed it must be remembered that in 1893 the Belfast Street Tramways Co had 800 horses working pulling double-decked tramcars on the granite square setts on the streets, in those days work for many farriers! I have mentioned the "Twin men of Iron" when the brothers retired they were presented with a television set by Thomas Wilson, a local farmer from the Mill on Ballylagan Road, from a grateful community. They lived for a number of years in retirement but Jeannie outlived them all, so long in fact, that no villager knew her age at all. In the 1971 census she enlisted the help of Davey Sempey, a neighbour always willing to help anyone, to fill in her census form and Davy naturally thought that he was the only person in the district who would know Jeannie s age. However when the form was filled in and all Jeanie had to do was to sign it and fill in her date of birth, she looked at Davy and in her lovely Ulster-Scots accent said to him Ach never mine, a ll finish the thing masel thus keeping her secret intact.

Thus from Straid passed the way the ringing of the anvil, the smell of burning hoof and above all the rattle of farm carts coming to the McCann's.

The only thing left of the Smithy today is the track of its roof left up against the Orange Hall gable and where it once stood is now incorporated in the Church Car Park.

The Simms family shown in the 1901 census

Ap.	Townlands and Occupiers.	Immediate Lessors.		Land. A.	R.	P.	£	s.	d.	Buildings. £	s.	d.
	SKILGANABAN—*continued.*											
b	Jane Baird,	Conway R. Dobbs,	Garden,	0	1	0	0	5	0	—		
			Total of Rateable Property,	566	0	15	416	13	0	36	7	
			EXEMPTIONS:									
b	. . . .	. . . .	National School-house,	—			—			0	10	
			Total, including Exemptions, .	566	0	15	416	13	0	36	17	
	STRAID. (*Ord. S. 46.*)											
a {	John Gamble, .	Marquis of Downshire, {	House, offices, and land,	41	2	0	27	10	0	2	10	
			Bog. . .	5	2	20	1	0	0	—		
1 *b*	Isaac Blackalder,	John Gamble, .	House and sm. garden,	—			—			0	10	
— *c*	William Bell, .	Same,	House and sm. garden,	—			—			0	5	
{	John Wilson. .	Marquis of Downshire, {	House, offices, corn-mill, kiln and land,	25	2	10	15	5	0	26	0	
			Land, . .	11	3	35	11	0	0	—		
			Land, . .	12	3	20	9	5	0	—		
{	Samuel Crowe, .	Same, . .	House, offices, & land, {	27	1	10	24	0	0	4	10	
				18	2	20	5	10	0	—		
				15	3	20	12	15	0	—		
{	Samuel M'Guiggan, .	Same, . .	Land, . . {	4	2	0	2	0	0	—		
				23	1	35	14	0	0	—		
7 A *a*	Hugh Miller, .	Samuel M'Guiggan, .	House, . .	—			—			0	10	
a {	Mary Wilson, .	Marquis of Downshire,	Ho., offs., shop, & ld., {	22	2	6	24	15	0	15	5	
				24	1	15	20	0	0	—		
9 *b*	James Hawthorne,	Mary Wilson, .	House, . .	—			—			0	15	
— *c*	Mary Adamson, .	Same, . .	House, . .	—			—			0	15	
— *d*	David Burns, .	Same, . .	House, . .	—			—			1	0	
— *e*	Andrew Johnston, .	Same, . .	House, . .	—			—			0	10	
{	John Boyd, .	Marquis of Downshire,	Land, . . {	2	2	35	2	15	0	—		
				8	2	30	4	10	0	—		
{	Samuel Logan, .	Same, . .	Land, . . {	4	1	5	4	5	0	—		
				7	3	25	3	15	0	—		
	James Boyd, .	Same, . .	Land, . .	7	2	5	6	5	0	—		
	William Hall, .	Same, . .	Ho., office, forge. & land,	6	3	30	5	15	0	4	0	
	Rev. James Bain,	Same, . .	Land, . .	12	0	30	8	15	0	—		
	Francis Jenkins, .	Same, . .	House, offices, and land,	24	0	30	20	5	0	3	10	
	Marquis of Downshire,	In fee, . .	Plantation, .	3	1	10	2	0	0	—		
{	Alexander Birnie,	Marquis of Downshire, {	House, offices, and land,	22	1	20	14	5	0	6	10	
			Land, .. .	24	0	30	7	0	0	—		
			Plantation, .	13	1	20	6	15	0	—		
	Wm. Stewart and Son,	Same, . .	House, offices, and land,	37	2	30	20	10	0	3	0	
	VILLAGE OF STRAID.											
1	Samuel M'Guiggan, .	Marquis of Downshire,	House, offices, and gar.	0	0	30	0	5	0	4	5	
2	Samuel Logan, .	Same, . .	House, office, and gar.	0	0	25	0	5	0	3	5	
3	James Boyd, .	Same, . .	House, offices, public-house and garden, . .	0	0	25	0	5	0	10	15	
4	Rev. James Bain,	Same, . .	House, offices, and gar.	0	1	10	0	10	0	6	10	
5	Presbyterian Meeting-house, and yard, .	(*See Exemptions.*)										
6	National School-house, and play-ground. .	(*See Exemptions.*)										
7	James Boyd, .	Marquis of Downshire,	Garden, . .	0	1	0	0	5	0	—		
8	Charles M'Manus, .	James Boyd, .	Ho., yard, and sm. gar.	—			—			0	15	
9	Samuel Bell, .	Same, .	Ho., yard, and sm. gar.	—			—			1	0	
10	John Boyd, .	Marquis of Downshire,	Ho., offs.. yd.,.& sm. gar.	0	0	7	—			1	15	
11	James Lennon, .	Same, .	House, off., and sm. gar.	0	0	8	—			1	5	
12	John Wilson (*lodgers*),	John Wilson, .	House, off., and sm. gar.	0	0	8	—			1	5	
13	Jane Wilson, .	Marquis of Downshire,	House, off., and sm. gar.	0	0	8	—			1	5	
14	Robert Scott, .	Same, .	House, and sm. garden,	0	0	8	—			1	0	
15	John Wilson, .	Same, .	Ho. (*in progress*) and gar.	0	0	38	0	5	0	—		
			Waste under houses, yards, streets, & small									

The County Antrim Farm Cart

The Carpenter

As said in the Chapter about the Blacksmith the two important men in the village were the Carpenter and the Blacksmith both equally important in the economy of any village and the surrounding area.

From the 1860 valuation carried out for the Government under the eye of a man called Griffith and being the first time that a tax, i.e. rates was imposed on the populace. Now-a-days with so much talk about the new building valuations of 2005 the people, especially farmers, were certainly worse off by this rate tax, as happens today, when a property was improved the valuation rises but up to the Gladstone Land Acts of the 1800 s all had to pay both the Government and the Landlord.

Thus we see from the Griffith Valuation for the Parish of Ballynure in 1860 the village of Straid had a James Lennon as Carpenter.

It must be remembered prior to the industrial revolution reaching Belfast the Carpenter had to fashion all timber to his needs including the intricate work of the wheelwright. When we remember that the ordinary wheel was made of three types of timber, ash for fellys (the rim of the cartwheel held in place by the spokes and banded together by the Iron tyre). Oak for the spokes to carry the weight and either elm or beech for the nave (hub) so that it does not split. All this timber including the planks of pine for the shafts and body was seasoned and completely dry and was in abundant supply around that time as the ships carrying emigrants to the the New World usually brought timber back in ballast for a speedy turn round and as the huge forests of North America were providing cheap timber the demand in Britain and Ireland was huge as the industrial Revolution required massive amounts of timber for factory buildings.

In examining the man-made spoked wheels. When one looked at a twelve spoked wheel from the front the wheel itself was absolutely perpendicular whereas the fourteen spoked wheel when viewed from the same angle was dished with the top spokes standing out at an angle of about 10 degrees But when the spoke was at the bottom it was absolutely vertical.

Imagine the intricate work in building this wheel as about 2 - 5∞ would result in its collapse. The author heard his father say many times that an expert carpenter when finishing the making of a cart when the hind door was on and fashioned it had to be without leaks when filled with water. The above watertight story leads me onto the task of the carpenter in making churns. There was the plunge churn and the larger churn made to be driven by a horse walking round in a circle outside the milk-house.

This circle was known as the churn walk and consisted of a round conical wheel lying horizontally with the base circumference being geared driving what was known as a drive shaft connected to a gear wheel on the churn to turn the paddles.

The churn itself was constructed like a huge wooden oblong box with a heavy brass tap at the front to draw off the buttermilk. A partition ran up the middle of the inside but Left a clear area front and rear so that the paddles swooshed the milk round in a circular motion to have it agitated to bring up the butter. The churn itself was constructed of yellow pine from North America (Pinus Rigida) and was the only known wood to have virtually no knots an attribute desirable when working with liquids. In the 1860's a gentleman called Arthur Griffith undertook a task to value every Property marked on the new Ordinance Survey maps which were created by the soldiers of the Royal Engineers from the 1830's.

On the Griffith valuation of the properties (enclosed) we find the name John Lennon (marked) who had rented from the Marquis of Downshire, the Landlord a small house With a notable valuation of £1.5.0d. And also had a garden of 8 perches. He was Straid's Carpenter and is mentioned as such in the Straid L.O.L. returns of the eighteen seventies.

We then go forward to the 1901 Census (enclosed) and find a Mary Simms, a widow having two sons, John and Samuel, being carpenters.

The last carpenter the author can trace in Straid is one John Clyde, presumably of the Clyde s of Seskin Brae.

Timber - the carpenters stock in trade.

Census of Ireland 1901, showing the two Simms brothers who were both carpenters.

Seskin Road where the Turk's body was found

The Great Turk Sensation

It was about nine of the clock on the morning of September 1931 that a local farmer, One James McCalmont, was driving his horse and cart from Straid over the Seskin Brae when, coming to about where the new Sitka fir trees were planted, his horse suddenly stopped and would not proceed or rusted as it is known in the equine world.

Seeing that the horse was keeping to one side of the road Mr McCalmont examined the opposite side and discovered to his horror a body, naked except for a women's bathing cap on its head, lying over a hedge.

Not wishing to disturb any evidence he immediately set off to Carrickfergus Police Station to report the finding. Upon the police shifting the corpse to the Mortuary a Dr.Grace Pollock pronounced death had taken place approximately ten hours previously due to two bullet wounds, one in the right temple and one in the right eye, inflicted with a .20 revolver. The victim was six feet two inches in height and appeared to be around 38 years old.

The theory of the police was that the body was brought to Seskin naked to thwart identification and the bathing cap to prevent blood staining a car.

By chance a suit of clothes and a bloodstained shoe were found in Church Lane in Belfast and the suit had been made in Instanbul. Along with the suit a newly repaired shoe was also found and as the body appeared to be that of a foreigner enquiries were shared between Detectives in Carrickfergus and Belfast.

A boot maker in the dockside area of Belfast recognised the shoe repair to be his and described a man measuring over six feet tall had the repair done, who spoke little English and was accompanied by a neat littler man wearing a beret.

In those days of relatively little crime this new piece of evidence was soon passed on and a woman appeared at Musgrave R.U.C. Station to say she and another girl had gone for a drive in a car with a small man, who was the driver, and when he went to get petrol the woman stated that a rubber bathing cap fell out of the dashboard pocket. She identified the bathing cap found on the dead man as the one she saw and also identified a photograph of the tall man.

With the help of the Metropolitan police and the passport authorities, an American citizen was arrested in London and charged in Carrickfergus on 16th September 1931 with the murder of Ahmed Musa, a native of Instanbul. He was Eddie Cullens.

The story then unfolded. Cullens, Musa and another Turk, Assam Redvan, had met in New York and formed a partnership to exploit as a freak a third Turk Zara Aga, whom they claimed to be the world's oldest man at 156.

Upon arrival in London in April 1931 they joined Bertram Mills Circus. On August 3oth 1931 Cullens and Musa left Liverpool by boat for Belfast where they hoped to show Zara Aga at some future date. They came with an Essex saloon car the property of Redvan.

Cullens signed his name in a lodging house as Berman Herman while Musa, who new very little English, did not register at all. Redvan who was sworn on the Koran told Detectives that when Cullens returned to the Circus at Leeds on September 6th he said that Musa remained in Belfast with a girl and had intended going with her to London.

From evidence it would appear that Musa and another Circus employee had a row and as he (Musa) had money saved it was likely that he would leave the Circus.

At the Winter Assizes in the County Court on the Crumlin Road in Belfast, Eddie Cullens was tried for the murder of Assam Musa starting on December 3rd.

The Attorney General, A B Babbington K.C. described the accused as a Cinema Machine Operator born of Jewish parents in Cyprus and now an American citizen.

An attractive young woman caused a sensation, known as Miss X, when she took the Witness Box, said she had received a letter from Cullens on September 10th 1931. This letter stated "We have fired the doctor because he tried to get fresh with "Sonny Boy". The "doctor" Miss X explained was Ahmed Musa and Sonny Boy was the old man Zara Aga.

A Liverpool Ironmonger gave evidence that Cullens had bought from him a pick, shovel and storm lamp (presumably a Hurrican Lamp) on August 23rd. Another witness stated that Cullens had a revolver in his room at Liverpool and that the lamp, pick and shovel were in a lock-up garage he had rented. The Prosecution's case put forward was that Cullens had intended to murder Musa in Liverpool but never had an opportunity to do so until he reached Belfast.

The motive was personal dislike, the robbery of Musa's money, some £72.00 and the fact that Zara Aga would be more valuable property if the profit was shared between two instead of three. Cullens listened unmoved when the Judge donned the Black Cap and pronounced the Death sentence.

Until his death, which took place on December 23rd, he maintained his innocence. An Appeal was heard but failed and subsequently he died on the scaffold by the hand of the executioner, Pierrepoint, on the 7th day of January 1932 with complete calmness and with a smile on his face.

Crumlin Road Jail, Belfast where Eddie Cullins, the murderer was hanged in 1932

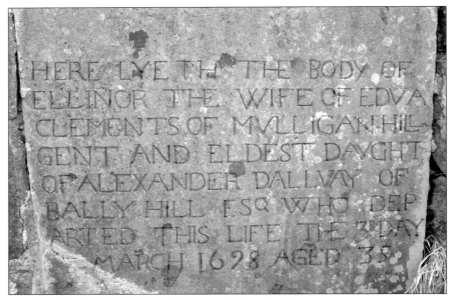

The Eleanor Clements tomb in Ballynure

Ellis, Clements and Crymble Families

Throughout the early history of Straid or Thomastown as it was then called (after a Thomas Stevenson of Carrickfergus who owned it prior to its coming into the County and town of Carrickfergus). The name of Ellis still appears after three hundred years, - in the new houses at the bottom of the street being called Ellisland Mews.

Robert Ellis was a Captain in the army and came to Ireland with Sir Hugh Clotworthy in the reign of Elizabeth I.

In 1681 he resided in Carrickfergus and in 1606-1607 he obtained Grants, forever, of two and a half shares of Corporation lands in the Middle Division.

He had three sons, John Edmund and Henry and in 1640 we find a Captain Henry Ellis commanding a Company of Irish soldiers at Newburn assisting the Scottish Covenanters.

This Henry also had issue and we find a Henry Ellis marrying Sarah, daughter of Edward Clements, Straid in 1711 but residing in Belfast.

This family of Clements came from Mulligan Hill but through the years the hill was changed to Clement's Hill and we find that Sarah's mother was the elder daughter of Alexander Dalway of Bellahill. A tablet flanks the sealed entrance to a basalt in Ballynure graveyard bearing the inscription: -

Here lyeth the body of Elinor, the wife of Edward Clements of Mulligan Hill,gent, and eldest daughter of Alexander Dalway of Bally Hill, Esq., who departed this life the 3rd day of March1628 aged 35 years.

There are two observations from the statement on the tablet, namely the first being the class Distinction, of one party being styled "gent" and the second "Esq".

But a more glaring fact has come to light. In all publications concerning Ballynure graveyard it has always been stressed that the Elinor Clements stone inscription is the oldest burial there, but in examination of the Dalway estate papers and confirming it in the edition (original) of Miskimmon's History of Carrickfergus it will be seen that Elinor Clements nee Dalway died in 1698 thus making all the writings about Ballynure graveyard wrong in the context of the oldest inscription.

However in returning to the Ellis family, Francis was Henry's brother and was a Captain in Sir John Clotworthy's Regiment and commanded the garrison in Antrim. He married Ann, Sister of Sir Hercules Langford of Langford Lodge, Crumlin and had four daughters. Mary the eldest was married to Theoppules Burleigh after whom Burleigh Hill on the Marshallstown Road, Carrickfergus is named and Susanna, another sister, married Hercules Clements.

We can see that the old families of the area all married amongst other and as a rule kept Estates among themselves.

Even the most established families of the time were in same part related to the Ellis family where we find Charles Adair of Loughanmore, (of the Adairs of Ballymena) married to Millicent Ellis in 1775.
The Crymble family resided between Straid lands and Clements Hill and of the three families less is known. They certainly kept up the tradition of marrying

into their own class as we find a Hercules Ellis who was a Captain in the army, and finding himself in Carrickfergus in 1760, apparently assisting in its defence against the French. Residing in Carrickfergus at Prospect, he married Catherine widow of the Rev. Robert Barry, daughter of Capt. Robert Adair, son of Sir Robert Adair of Ballymena. After his death his brother Henry inherited Prospect, was Mayor of Carrickfergus several times and married Elinor, daughter of Waterhouse Crymble of Clements Hill and had three girls and one boy Henry.

From the M.S. records of Carrickfergus and MSS of the Langford family we find a Hercules Ellis married Susanna a niece of Sir Hercules Langford of Langford Lodge and sold property to a John Clements, a son of Edward of Little Ballymenagh (old spelling) which he subsequently foolishly sold to Charles Crymble of Ballygallogh for "a song, and an old horse and £10.00 in hand".

Thus from the above we see a female Crymble lived on the Ellis estate whose entrance is still seen at the corner of the Woodburn and Ballynure Roads, Carrickfergus and was latterly owned by the family and a plaque placed there by the Carrickfergus Borough Council tells us that the 3rd Brigade of the Belgium Forces received their training here prior to the Invasion of France on 6th June 1944.

Woodburn entrance to Prospect Estate owned by Henry Ellis

The O'Haughins

All during my boyhood years my father would regale me with stories about the outlaw gang whose exploits terrorised the community from the Braid to Carrickfergus in the first half of the eighteenth century and not until I started to research County Court records of that era did I find this folklore, which had been handed down through the generations, was substantially true.

It would appear that around 1710 a small farmer in Braid was making a living and had four sons and it happened that on reaching manhood these sons turned out ne'er-do-wells.

Their names were Roger, Eneas or Nees (in English), John   and Shane Oge. They also had a foster brother Philemy. Rearing five boys would keep any family poor but instead of helping on the farm the brothers roamed about the neighbourhood and were engaged in poaching, cockfighting and other lawless pursuits leading to the aged father taking it to heart and falling into serious debt to the landlord and was eventually given notice of eviction. It must be remembered here that at that given period, there was no police force in the land

and not until 1787 was there an introduction of an armed Police Force and Bailiffs had a free hand in evictions. When the Bailiffs appeared on the farm intent on eviction a melee resulted in which one of them suffered a fatal blow, fell and never rose again. As all the brothers had been implicated all fled the scene and warrants were issued against them all. After placing their old father in a hovel near Sherrywherry they joined a party of notorious outlaws under the leadership of a certain Captain McCalister and were dreaded by the peaceful inhabitants of the most of East Antrim. When Captain McCalister was finally caught by the Army and executed, the Army being responsible for the law, Nees, one of the O'Haughin brothers was elected leader and started to terrorise the area.

One of the chief places of refuge of this band was near a small tributary of the Glenwhirry River near Donaghy's bridge where there were a number of caves; another lawless place frequented was the King's Moss near Ballyclare. The caves at the Knockagh, Greenisland are still there at a place named Archy's bushes.

On one occasion after a night of robbery and plunder the gang went to a shebeen between Teenies and Buckna and in the middle of the festivities a posse of Braid men who had been alerted by their presence fell upon them whereupon they scattered but rallied at the top of the hill near Tennies and put up such a determined defence that the Braid men withdrew but not before a bullet nicked one of them in the ear. This man was called Allen and, of course, as happened in those days when all escapades were set down in poems and the last two verses of an existing poem go thus

Range round your Chief, my men

These are but shabby fellows

We'll fight them one to ten

Ere we swing on the gallows

With that came whizzing thro' the air

A bullet from the callan

That carried off the ear

Of singing Rabin Allen.

Shortly after this episode due to a purge of the mounted cavalry from Carrick Castle sweeping the gangs usual haunts some were captured, others escaped, chief of same being Shane Oge. It appears to me that the word "Oge" meaning in Irish "young" was probably given to him to. distinguish him from Shane Senior.

This Shane Oge had great strength and courage and was proportionately generally feared by the populace but his ready wit ensured him to be able to scrape through many traps laid for him.

That he was not totally evil can be borne out by two instances that occurred, one in the King's Moss and the other in the town land of Brantang near Ballynure. It can readily be acknowledged, that a person living as Shane Oge did below the open sky and the stars, would eventually fall ill and it is thought that he developed pneumonia and called with a small farmer for shelter. In admitting this sick stranger to his home the farmer had a shrewd suspicion who his guest was and, in settling him down discovered he was carrying a horse pistol and thought that discretion was the better part of valour. After careful nursing and good wholesome food Shane Oge left the small farm in King's Moss much to the farmer and families relief.

Imagine the farmer's surprise when, answering a thump on his door late one April evening after dark, he saw the previously sick large man on his doorstep. After admittance and partaking something to eat the stranger enquired if everything was all right on the farm and was shocked to learn the farmer was in bad arrears in his rent to Lord Donegal and that the Lord's agent would be calling on the 1st May when the rent was due and that certain eviction would follow if the rent was not forthcoming.

Upon Shane Ogle telling the sceptical farmer to stop worrying and that he would see him right he left and returned on 11th night of May (by the Julian calendar, as the Gregorian calendar was not introduced in Britain and the English colonies until 1752) and handed over more gold sovereigns than were needed for the present rent plus the arrears. It came as no surprise to the farmer when he learned that the Lord's land agent had been waylaid and robbed on 12th night along with his rent and a lot of other farmers' rent as well.

It was about this time that Shane Oge was returning on foot from Glenwhirry when crossing over the Ollar river (Now the Sixmile Water) when he was spotted by some farmers who soon formed a posse on horseback and set off in pursuit. Seeing them catching up upon him from an advantage point at

Dickeystown Ballyeaston, he saw the farmer after whom the town land was named carrying sheaves of corn from a stack into a barn and he immediately stripped to his shirt sleeves and joined in, with the posse passing without a glance.

It was shortly after this when Shane Oge stood on the high ground around Knockagh and watched Philemy, his foster brother and the sole remainder be taken in a cortage to the Three Sisters, the gallows on the Belfast Road at Carrickfergus and hanged.

It is on record that shortly afterwards, Shane Oge, with a companion, went to a house in the town land of Bryantang, near Ballynure, where an old couple by the name of Scott lived together, and reputed to be very rich but very Godly.

At this point as my name is Scott and I was born and reared in Bryantang, I make no claim by being descended from this couple on two accounts. I am neither Godly nor rich, but Shane Oge creeping up to the old couple's door heard the old man praying for mankind including the poor, those who had nowhere to lay their head and the outcast who everyone hunted. At this stage he returned to his companion and informed him that no one would harm the Godly old man and woman and that the word would be spread amongst the lawless community that no harm was to befall them.

In spite of the army and being hunted by many farmers' posse's Shane Oge was never caught but was betrayed by a kinsman. His wife was a McKinstry and she had a brother called Shemus Bawn, because of his dark complexion, and all were celebrating New Year's Eve in a house owned by a man called Murphy when the poteen must have had an effect and Shemus Bawn and Shane Oge had high words, he intimated that the McKinstry clan "sprang from beggars base and wandering gipsy brood". After the party broke up Shane Oge went to Magherabawn to a cave and word had got out about the party and men from the Braid informed by Shemus Bawn, where Shane Oge had gone to rest, arrived at Magherabawn where McKinstry had led them and who now was with Shemus Bawn telling him that his wife, Shane's sister had taken ill and would he come and see her.

In following McKinstry at a place called Killylane Steps, Shane was alerted to danger and was usual in rural areas a poem was written immediately after the event which describes the foul deed more eloquently than I could put into words. The last two and half verses go thus:

"McKinstry halt" at length he cries
And leans him 'gainst a stone
"Some lurking foe before us lies
Just now a weapon shone",
Once more his eye glanced o'er the plain
His friend a broad axe drew
And says "Betide what will, dear Shane
I'll live or die with you".

But Oh! Accursed be he who thus spake
Accursed his hour of birth
For with one furious savage stroke
He smote him to the earth
The ambush men, with loud hurrah
Rush up with whirlwind speed
And bind his limbs while yet he lay
Unconscious of the deed.

To prison strong and certain death
They march at funeral pace
The last and boldest ere trod heath
O' famed O'Haughins race.

There is no doubt that the end of the O'Haughins reign of lawlessness and rapine was of great benefit as a whole to the East Antrim area, yet even to this day, something mean and dishonourable like treachery, is frowned upon as we in the past have known informers to be executed by paramilitaries.

The above McKinstry was forced to leave Glenwherry and seek asylum in the Braid where he eked out a living as a Thatcher and was a figure of derision and scorn.

The above story is told in full in a little book published in 1843 by a schoolmaster; Samuel Turner from Ballycorr, Ballyclare, called "Gleanings from Ballyboley Braes" and a commemorative plaque to his writings is to be seen in Ballyclare Town Hall.

The following is the Ulster-Scots rendering of what the
Straid congregation would have heard 191 years ago from
Rev. Bain
Translated by the Author

oooOOOooo

THE GOOD SHEPHERD

Wha is my Shepherd weel a ken
The Lord Hisell is he

He leads me whaur the girse is green
An' burnies quaet that be
Aft times I fain astray wud gang
An' wanner far awa'
He fins me oot, He puts me right
'An brings me hame an' a'
Though I pass through the gruesom' sheugh
Fin a ken he is near
His muckle crook will me defen'
Sae I hae nought tae fear
Ilk comfort whilk a sheep cud need
His thoughtfu' care provides
Though wolves an' dugs may prowl aboot'
In safety me He hides
His guidness an' His mercy baith
Nae doot will bide wae me
While faulded on the fields o' time
His hame my dwelling be.

Straid Church

This lovely little church stands at the corner of the Irish Hill Road, formerly the Belfast Road, and Main Street. It is built in a cruciform fashion with a centre aisle and a wing on each side. A tablet on the church gable, facing Main Street, has the inscription "Ebenezer, erected 1816, rebuilt and enlarged 1857.

Ebenezer to my mind, and I am open to correction, was probably the term of religion used before the church changed the name to the Independent Church as it was when the first minister we can record, a James Bain was called and ordained by the Church. Sometime during the Rev. Bain's ministry, which lasted 43 years, the form of congregationalism as it is today came about. This type of holy worship is the doctrine of a Protestant evangelical and Trinitarian Church based on a form of government, which began in England in 1567 and gained strength.

The first minister we can find on the records was this James Bain whose influence had a marked effect on the congregation in that during the 43 years ministry, we find not only the Church flourishing but also being rebuilt and enlarged in 1857.

In a time of hardship just before the rising of employment in the Belfast Shipyards, Linen Mills and Rope Works, all of which later in the century would become the largest in the world, help was given in money by Mrs Jane Clements Nicholey (see old families of Straid in this book) whose father Captain Henry Ellis gave assistance to the founding of the original church in 1816.

Great credit must be given to the founders at that time because the Battle of Waterloo had only taken place one year previously and as always a slump occurred when hostilities ceased and armies disbanded as happened after W.W.I. but fortunately not after the second world war as agricultural prices were held up by guarantee.

During the Rev. James Bain's stewardship, as well as improving church property his evangelical prowess is very obvious. Just before renovations began in 1857 he held six open-air meetings in the summer and we find one of these meetings in 1853 attracted over 400 people attending.

As has been stated Rev. Bain's sojourn in Straid lasted 43 years and he, no doubt, could be claimed to be the founding father of Straid Congregational.

Many must have wished Rev. Bain had still been in harness when we study the number of clergymen who served Straid from 1880 at the end of Rev. Bain's ministry. For the next 48 years until 1929 when the Rev.Samuel Duff was called to the ministry, 12 Ministers had an average stay of 4 years, three of them, Rev. W Hughes, Rev. F H Baird, Rev. T J Forsythe staying only two years and another, Rev. J E Reilly residing one year.

The earliest Straid Minister the author can recall was Rev. Samuel Duff who arrived in 1929 and stayed until 1940 when he had a call to Templepatrick Presbyterian Church, "call" being a euphemism for a minister going to another church at the behest of the other congregation although the author has seldom heard of a clergyman getting a "call" to a poorer congregation. Rev. Duff was well-liked in Straid having at that time two sisters living in Ballynure and he was a mild mannered little man whose sole aim was to keep in touch with his flock by visiting them.

Rev. Duff left Straid during what is now termed "the phoney war" when hostilities had not yet begun in the Netherlands and Rev. James Brooks, who had preached in both Richill and Donaghy, Co Tyrone came to take over the task of steering his flock through four years of a terrible world war in which men from Straid were fighting. His previous experience in Home

The Rev. James Brooks

42

Missions stood him in good stead as we find him on the Executive Committee of the Irish Union and from 1949 –1956 he was Chairman of the Congregational Union of Ireland. After 16 years in Straid he moved to Peterhead, Aberdeenshire for a number of years and retired to Helensburgh

Straid Boy's Brigade showing the Rev. Brooks as Captain and Hugh Greer, Lieutenant circa 1950   R. Ferguson collection.

Dumbartonshire where he was eventually laid to rest. In 1957 Rev. George Trimble, who incidentally stayed 16 years as did his predecessor, and like all incumbents of the position left his mark. We find that in 1972 there was one of Straid congregation's Gift Sundays at which £420.00 was lifted, a very significant sum in those days.

On September 3rd 1971 a very large turn out was evident in Straid at the Annual Missionary Conference and another significant took place in 1969 when after many years, a son of the Manse married. Rowland George Trimble married Margaret Simms in Abbotscross Congregational Church.

At the Rev. Trimble's retirement function he, Mrs Trimble and second son Trevor were presented with gifts. R H Stewart of Belfast, a member of the Congregational Union of Ireland presided and Wm. John Weatherup, on behalf of the Deacons and Committee handed over a gold watch to Mr Trimble while Mrs David Jenkins presented Mrs Trimble with a silver tea service, Miss Jane Ferguson also presented a travelling clock to Trevor.

John Dunn, senior deacon also paid tribute and a musical evening followed given by the Church Choir.

In 1973 Rev. Ronnie McCracken took up the Church Stewardship but only sojourned 4 years but was extremely busy with missionary work. He led the Harvest Service in 1973 in the Commons School (now closed) and at his first Harvest Service in Straid, Jean Wilson and Sandra Weatherup were the soloists with Miss May Patterson at the organ.

At a time of having little ready cash to spend it is perhaps now-a-days hard for our youth to understand how the nights of those days were spent. In the winter the Young Farmers' Club took up our energy but surprising enough for a month and a half all would attend harvest thanksgiving services over a wide area.

The author well remembers the harvest services in Straid even long before 1973 and what sticks in his mind was the fact that every year, without fail, the closing praise was always John Ellerton's lovely evening hymn "The day thou gavest Lord is ended" and it was only later in his life he equated the words with Psalm 113 verse 3 which states "From the rising of the sun unto the going down of the same the Lord's name is to be praised".

On Rev. McCracken's departure the Rev. Noel Darragh arrived and already has had 29 most successful years to his credit and one would sincerely hope he would break Rev. Bain's record of 43 years.

His Reverence was born in the town land of Fern, Co Donegal bordering the Co Tyrone town of Castlederg and brought up on a farm where he developed his interest in farm animals especially horses and sheepdogs. His horse riding proficiency today was learned on the back of a donkey!

The family then moved across the border to a farm near Sion Mills, Co Tyrone and at 18 years of age trusted the Lord as his Saviour.

He married the girl next door (lucky for him he flitted) in 1968 and spent five years on a small farm in the town land of Droit, between Gortin and Newtownstewart. After the birth of two children (Noeleen and Stephen) he decided to take up full Christian work and left farming to go to Emmanuel Bible College in Birkenhead. He spent six years there and in 1972 he answered a call to Straid Congregational Church and immediately fitted into farming and the country life again.

It is a measure of the man that since arriving in Straid, land was bought and a complete lovely big Manse was built while the old Manse adjoining the Church was converted into a beautiful large hall for all the Church activities.

Being an energetic man as well as carrying out his pastoral duties to the full he always has had time to train his horses and keep his sheepdog busy among his flock. He is following in the footsteps of the clergymen of old who had smallholdings to augment their stipend – the only difference being, his work is a hobby.

He is not the Minister of Agriculture but rather the agricultural minister and

The field above Straid Manse, Seskin Road

well liked and respected as such. Out of the few Clergymen I could count on one hand whom I hold in the greatest esteem, the Rev Noel Darragh comes high on the list, and his wife I hold in the same category. I feel that if they left Straid after 29 happy years their hearts would somehow be back on the Seskin Road.

As a footnote to things ecclesiastical I would suppose not many in East Antrim below the age of 50 would realise that within two miles of Straid a Roman Catholic Chapel celebrated Mass until 1962.

Leaving Straid and proceeding up the Seskin Road towards Carrickfergus a traveller after less than two miles comes to a staggered cross roads, the right hand one being the Lisglass Road and the other Councillors Road, 100 yards below the entrance to Councillors Road stands Woodburn Presbyterian Church. In a small field 300 yards from Woodburn Church on the Straid side stood a small Chapel, called St Colmcille's Church built in 1882 and celebrating the last Mass on 1st April 1962. It then stood derelict until it was demolished in 1987 the stones being used to build Carrickfergus Marina.

St. Colmcille's Church, Woodburn. Built in 1882.

The building of this small Chapel was directly due to circumstances in Belfast at that time. Although Belfast did not officially become a City until Queen Victoria granted that status in 1888 by Charter it was the third largest port on the United Kingdom with a population of 174,412 in 1871. This posed many problems for the Town Council at that time mainly the supply of clean drinking water to the populace. In 1865 a body called the Belfast Water Commissioners laid down plans to dig dams in Carrickergus area for storage and three dams were dug above Woodburn, one at Marshallstown and another, the North Dam, on the New Line to Ballynure.

Hundreds of navvies from Counties Donegal and Londonderry were brought in to the Carrickfergus area to dig these dams out with spade and shovel with local farmers using horses and carts to carry the soil to build the banks.

The reason for the name of St Colmcille's leads the author to suspect that in deference to the area these men, some with their families came from, the Patron Saint of the North West of old Ulster was St. Colmcille.The hard work and the engineering feats of the day are still plain to be seen and the plantation of all the spruce and pine trees in the Carrickfergus area are a direct result of the efforts of these men.

The make of the religion of these men was generally Roman Catholic and it is a tribute we owe to the Belfast Water Commissioners who saw the religious needs of their workers and provided a place of worship for them.

Class of 1935 - R. Ferguson collection

Education in Straid

The first school in Straid, apart from the hedge schools of the late 1700's and early 1800's, was set up in the middle of the village through the munificence of one lady, namely Jane Anne Clements Nicoley who lies at rest in Ballynure Graveyard.

Who was this lady? Where did she get the money not only for the school but also gave money to found Straid's only church? One thing is sure she came from a wealthy family.

There is one short history of the Ellis family elsewhere in this book but it is worthwhile delving into the ancestry of Jane who was the last remaining representative of that family.

A Henry Clements Ellis was Mayor Carrickfergus from 1754 –1757 and again in 1793, hence Ellis Street in Carrickfergus, and he married Elinor, a daughter of Waterhouse Crymble of Clements Hill, Straid and had three daughters and one son, also Henry, who inherited Straid land on the death of his uncle Edward Crymble and married firstly Jane, daughter of William Burleigh of

Dublin who died in 1795 without issue. His second wife was also a Jane, daughter of James Craig of Carrickfergus and the issue from that marriage was also Jane who firstly married Duncan Wilson and secondly Christian William Nicoley.

Thus Jane Nicoley became the last remaining representative of a very old and noble family whose presence around Straid today is not appreciated.

From the small school she set up on Main Street, presumably near the Mansion House of her Grandfather, mentioned elsewhere, in 1828 measuring 32 x 16 feet, it continued until an organisation called The Kildare Place Society came into being.

During the first half of the 19th century mass education and increasing literacy was spreading throughout Ireland and in 1824 a Commission was appointed into the general state of Irish education. The oldest Society which was engaged in elementary education was the Incorporated Society for Promoting English Protestant Schools in Ireland and was founded in 1733 but an organisation known as the Kildare Place Society founded in Dublin in 1811 and was also known as the Society of the Poor in Ireland. This organisation offered the best educational services and was managed by a committee of people from different religious persuasions and as the Government was committed to a policy of integration, various factors made the Society subject to Roman Catholic hierarchy. However, the Government had to abandon an attempt to make it, by means of a grant, the channel for assisting primary education. In 1831 a system that was known as the National Education Act came into being and a grant of £30,000 was made by the Kildare Place Society to a Band of Commissioners who were to help build and repair school houses and make grants for the payment of teachers and provision of text books.

A stone, lime and slate schoolhouse in Straid was built by public subscription on the Carrickfergus Road (now the Seskin Road) in 1847 (incidentally the worst year of the Great Famine telling us that the Straid area was reasonably unaffected).

It contained two adjoining rooms each 16' x 10' for male and female. The Rev. James Bain of the Straid Independent Church in the village applied to connect the School to the National Board set up by the aforementioned Kildare Place Society and was successful on 26th February 1848.

The first teacher was a John Walker, aged 44, who had a licence to teach given under the hand and seal of the Lieutenant Governor of New Brunswick, Canada in 1838 at an annual salary of £20.00 (Emigration in reverse?).

The population can be judged in those days by the fact that within a radius of two and a half miles of Straid, seven schools were in operation, namely Ballylaggan, Ballynarry, Ballynure, Skilganaban, Bruslee, Straidnahanna and Aldoo.

We find in 1862 a teacher called Samuel Hadden attained 3.1Classification only during his 12 years at Straid and was found by the Inspector to be a reasonable teacher![1]

Prior to Hadden's appointment Straid Male School was struck off grant aid because of the low state of the building and re-instatement was attained and both male and female rooms were extended to 22' x 16' x 10'. The re-instatement was attained through the efforts of Rev. Bain and Inspector Irvine reported, "all conditions improvements made[2]".

But what about the female schools?

A report of Head Inspector P J Keenan on Straid Female School in October 1855 states "Under the same roof as the boy's school. Satisfactory as to maps, tablets (Slates), blackboard etc.

Time Table not precise enough, accounts correct, school neat and tidy and orderly, children very clean, discipline good. This is a useful little school. Not a bad report!"

Marg Wilson won a Premium for Order in 1855 after six years of good service[3]. Mary Craig left for Australia in 1860, and Margaret Patten was Principal from 1861 –1874. With an average daily attendance of 27 in 1870 the average contribution per child in fees during the year was two shillings and eight pence.

1. Inspectors District BookED5/1/1P.5
2. Grant Aid application EDI/5/.P.84
3. Commissioners Report ED1/3/P.67. PRONI.

There seems to be a gap in detail about Straid Male and Female until we find a new school had been built on the Belfast Road, (now the Irish Hill Road) and the renowned James Sloan was Principal. This was just after the disastrous first world war and pupil numbers had tumbled due to the families moving to Belfast for work in the shipyard, linen mills and all the industries required for the war effort. This James Sloan was one of a rare breed that knew instinctively the ability of his pupils and indeed two turned into imminent surgeons another of the same family an expert on tropical diseases and spent most of her life in tropical Africa. Another pupil became Professor of Theology in the Presbyterian Church and many, if not all were a success in their chosen walks of life.

The work of James Sloan took its toll on his appearance however if one examines the first photograph herein with him standing in the rear to the left of the picture (circa 1920) and hosting a fine head of black hair and find him in photograph No.2 sitting in the front (circa 1926) still with a full head of hair but Persil white.

He was a strict disciplinarian and many hands smarted in the process. His assistants were firstly Miss Robson and his daughter Jenny while Eleanor Sloan (no relation) was a monitor and then went down to Ballynure Public Elementary School as an assistant to Robert J Wilson who followed James Courtney as principal with Mrs Courtney junior teacher. This was circa 1935.

James Sloan retired prior to the outbreak of war in September 1939 and the post was filled by S Windrum Armour, popularly known as Windy, whose forte was, apart from teaching, a great believer in organising the youth of the district, so much so he founded and helped the Straid Young Farmers' Club during his period of teaching.

All during the war we find in perusing the Larne Times, we read of the efforts of Mr Armour in all the aspects of helping the War effort . In 1944 he was appealing to the public to put greater effort into buying War Savings Certificates and later he was to be found heading an organisation called the War Land Advisory Service.

S Windrum Armour continued in this vein until about 1948, a Wm. James Beggs of Carrickfergus took his place and continued in the post until 1975, twenty-seven and a half years dedication to the pupils of Straid and a valuable member of the Young Farmers Club.

Compare Principal James Sloan's hair in the two pictures!

After his sojourn with the young of Straid he decided to attend Theological College and became a Presbyterian Minister and the author would have liked to ask him which was the most stressful – listening to a room full of boisterous pupils or ministering to a congregation who, like the pupils, wished he would stop talking and let them go home.

During Billy Beggs stewardship there was an assistant teacher who for many years taught Irish Dancing and turned out many pupils with outstanding deportment and poise. Her name was Betty McCullough (married name Mrs. K. Greer) and she was successful in turning out prizewinners at the many musical festivals of that time under her tuition in the Ashleigh Dance Club in Ballyclare.

The next three Principals were, in turn, Mr B Evans, Mr T Leathem and a Mr Cromie who left in 1999 and was succeeded by Mrs Florence Mairs under whose stewardship the school has prospered and advanced dramatically. It had been completely rebuilt and refurbished in 1953 and was deemed to be large enough but, due to the expansion of building houses around Straid numerous temporary class rooms have had to be added on.

One of the many good points Mrs Mairs possesses is a fondness for teaching local history and has many times has steered her pupils towards winning competitions and has done more than any teacher to bring the school's reputation to the fore.

It is perhaps ironic to find that Straid school with a roll of circa., 87 pupils is now in 2007 on the list of schools being considered for closure and indeed in my estimation would be a total disaster for the whole area of Straid and its hinterland and one sincerely hopes that Mrs Mairs and her excellent staff may continue to impart their expertise to the young.

Straid has been lucky in having good education, good salvation in the Church and no damnation at all due to the local hostelry being closed in 1921.

STRAID P.E. SCHOO

PUPILS' WAR EFFORT

ENJOYABLE SPORTS FOLLOW

On Wednesda; of last week, pri the break-up of Straid P.E. Schoo the summer holidays, an interesting gramme of sports was carried throu a field kindly lent by Mr. R. H. W J.P., chairman of the school committe

During the past three months the p have worked with a fine patriotic and much enthusiasm in collecting a amount of scrap paper and metal as contribution in helping to win the The sale of this scrap provided ref ments and prize-money at the sports in addition made available to each attending school a small sum of mor

The sports were organised by principal Mr S. Windrum Armour, a an interval refreshments were serve Miss I. M. Sloan, the assistant tea assisted by Mr. Willoughby Wilson. following are the results of the va events :—

100 Yards.—Boys (5-8 years)—1, Jenkins; 2, John Blair. Girls (5-8 y —1, Sally Cowden; 2, Sheila H Boys (8-11 years)—1, Dixon Boyd; 2, Hunter. Girls (8-11 years)—1, Hunter; 2, Molly Logan. Boys years)—1, Joe Greer; 2, Eric Hu Girls (11-14 years)—1, Sadie Haga Nellie Hall.

220 Yards.—Junior boys—1, J Wilson; 2, Samuel Kennedy. Senior —1, Ian Wilson; 2, Eric Hunter. J girls—1, Betty Hunter; 2, Sheila Hu Senior girls—1 Sadie Hagan; 2, Cowden.

Three-Legged Race.—Junior bo Dixon Boyd and Robert M'Lean. S boys—1, W. Cowden and W Vint. J girls—1, M. Cooke and M. Dunbar. S girls—1. G. Montgomery and H. Park

Potato Race.—Junior boys—1, K. I gomery; 2, J. Jenkins. Senior boys— Millar; 2, W. Vint. Junior girls—1, Logan; 2, Betty Hunter. Senior gir Margaret Logan; 2, Nellie Hall.

One-Legged Race.—Junior boys— M'Lean; 2, D. Boyd. Senior boys— Wilson; 2, D. Henderson. Junior gir Shelia Hunter; 2, Molly Logan. S girls—1, Sadie Hagan; 2, H. Park.

Gas Mask Race.—Junior boys— Jenkins; 2, K. Montgomery. Senior —1, D. Henderson; 2, Ian Wilson. J girls—1, Sheila Hunter; 2 S. Co Senior girls—1, H. Park; 2, A. Gree

Obstacle Race.—Senior boys— Millar; 2, Robert Wilson. Junior gir M. Dunbar; 2, S. Hunter. Senior gir Margaret Logan; 2, A. Greer.

Long Jump.—Junior Boys—1, R. M 9 years (12ft 3ins.); 2, J. Montgo Senior boys—1, R. Ferguson, 13 years 10ins.); 2, I. Wilson, 11 years (13ft. Junior girls—1, S. Cowden, 8 years 8ins.); 2, M. Logan. Senior girls— Hall, 11 years (11ft. 1in.); 2, H. Par years (11ft, 7ins.).

High Jump.—Senior boys—1, J. J (3ft. 9ins.); 2, W. Vint (3ft. 8ins.). Girls' relay race—J. Moore, S. J E. Cooke and Sally Cowden.

Boys' Relay Race—Eric Hunter, Wilson, R. M'Lean, Robert Wilson. The winning team, captained by Millar, had 62 points.

Straid School Sports Day 1942

Musings

It is with a great deal of pleasure and much nostalgia I look back to when I was a boy in 1938 and the first battalion of the Welsh Regiment had summer camp in east Antrim.

Half of the battalion roughly 350 men were encamped in tents surrounding the mill dam on the Ballylagan Road while the other half were in Ballynure where Castletown Park is now with many stationed in the beetling mill which ceased working in 1936 and the rest in Nissan huts which the Engineers hurriedly erected.

Little did the populace realise at that time the purpose of the camp was a ruse to send out working parties to find out the state of the road bridges for carrying tanks and heavy transport.

The hint of an impending war at that time, before the Prime Minister, Neville Chamberlain returned from Munich with his infamous paper saying "Peace in our time" was very prevalent.

Little did the locals and indeed the troops themselves know that within one and a half years many would be dead and many captured at Dunkirk.

The Regimental Band was in tents in Straid and two things stick in my memory quite clearly. After all these years, 69 to be precise, I can recall very clearly the Bandmaster's name, Major Doubt, who visited my parents regularly and looked splendid in his blue uniform with a broad red stripe down the outside of his trouser legs.

In an effort to win hearts and minds of the populace the Band would give performances in both Straid and Ballynure to which everyone was invited and on Sunday many would parade to the local churches. Best of all was the official marches in both villages with a huge he-goat leading the Band as the Battalion mascot. Covering the goat was a purple vest with the Royal Arms on the right hand side and a huge leek depicted on the other.

To the Regimental March, Men of Harlech, the Band made a wonderful sight and many chests swelled with pride as in those days many were proud to belong to the British Empire.

I remember well Major Doubt bringing a message from the Commanding Officer to my father, asking if it would be possible to allow troops to come and carry stones out of the Ballylagan burn across one of my father's fields to stack as the weather was fine. Having gained permission about 50 troops arrived next day and denuded the burn of every stone in it, much to my father's satisfaction. Imagine his fury when he discovered the order had been given to replace every stone that night! What he did not know at the time was that another 50 troops turned up the next day and repeated the process and did so until every soldier in the Battalion, Officers excluded, had a turn which took a fortnight, Sundays excluded.

He, my father, never did get the burn free of stones as the last batch was dumped all back in again. It had never occurred to him that this was the only way of relieving boredom for those not engaged in training.

Another fond memory from those days was the presence of what was known as "surface-men" on the roads then being kept in order by the County Councils. These roadmen, as they were also called, had a pride in their work and were experts in using three hand implements, which, in the main, the present day worker has forgotten how to use.

Tied to their bicycles were a scythe, a cutting hook, a spade and a brush while across the handlebars was a skein of heavy cord between two pieces of iron pegs to drive into the roadside to make a straight line. This line was laid up the side of the road and the spade was used to make a tidy verge at the side of the road, which was then swept clean with the brush. This was winter work when the verges were soft and in summer the scythe and hook kept the bunkers clean.

In Main Street, Straid there lived one of these roadmen, a John McLean, whose workmanship on the local roads was outstanding but heaven help the hapless farmer with horse and cart who, in John's sight let the wheel of the cart over-run the verge and destroy his work.

To a small boy in the blazing hot summer days of the nineteen-thirties the arrival of the tar boiler on the roads was a red-letter event. This machine was just a huge square steel box with an iron wheel on each corner into which was incorporated a coal firebox at the bottom that heated the tar in the box above. Glutinous tar was fed into the boiler from a forty-five gallon barrel and was transferred through to waiting watering cans with a sheet of tin fitted horizontally across the tip to spread the tar on the road. Behind all this came a lorry with three quarter inch screenings, which were then spread on top of the tar. When these screenings were eventually flattened through wear and tear the tar in those days in very sunny weather bubbled to the surface and I well remember walking with my classmates from Ballynure Public Elementary School, as it was then called to the Craig Hill in Ballyclare in 1935 to celebrate the Silver Jubilee of King George V and the tar sitting in bubbles in the road and by me having as usual my stockings hanging over my boots and in short trousers my legs were covered in tar and in those far off days butter was the only thing my mother had to clean me up. It is also incredible in these days of medical awareness to remember that parents with children with a malady called croup, an inflammation of the larynx and trachea, brought them and made the poor unfortunates breath in the thick acrid fumes from the boiling tar as a cure. Now we have a smoking ban to protect both smoker and passive smoker from breathing in tar!

While mentioning the nineteen thirties it is perhaps time to mention the weather in both summer and winter in these times of wet summers and frost free winters. I can well remember the icicles hanging from roofs at least a foot and a half long in a period of very frosty weather and usually when snow fell it froze and lay on the ground for weeks on end. When wakening up in bed in the mornings the windows were completely opaque with frost and the last thing one wanted to do was to come out of a warm bed and put bare feet on the cold linoleum. It was warmer standing on the bare boards of the floor and usually one could see every breath condensing in the cold air. Little did I know that I was privileged to even have linoleum on the bedroom floor.

Being reared beside a fresh water lake of twenty four acres which was quite deep in places summer time was a pleasure indulged in boating, fishing and swimming but those winter days on that dam, covered in ice to a depth of six inches and more was a pleasure with ones pals. Bicycles were ridden all over the ice and I well remember a Major and Mrs McCance, owners of the local mill in Ballyclare called The Green, telling me that when the solid ice was cracking that was the time it was safe to skate as when water froze there was a vacuum between it and the ice but when the ice cracked it settled down and was supported by the water. It was a wonder that none of us were drowned.

In a time of easy comfortable living with electricity, central heating, carpets, television and now mobile phones, one who has been used to these conveniences and maybe been used to nothing else may find it hard to believe how we used to be able to wash, dress and polish ones shoes in the dark. There was usually only one lamp per household and another used outside to look after the cattle, usually a Tilley with a mantle, which had to be handled carefully as it was fragile.

Indeed in those days males wore shirts with detached collars held by two collar studs and I well remember that, when dressing to go out to a Young Farmers Club dance, if I dropped a stud I had no trouble finding it in the dark while now I can hardly enter a room without turning on the electricity.

Young people may ask nowadays what we did in the summer when there was no refrigeration? Then the only way we had was a fine meshed box bolted onto a north facing wall in which to keep meat and perishables such as butter and lard and I might say that in the main we had no trouble spreading our butter. Speaking of lard brings to mind pig slaughtering on the farm, a practice now forbidden and my mother rendering the pig fat into lard and boiling the head of the a pig which we were going to preserve in salt, the head being made into brawn a delicious filling for sandwiches, which I remember well devouring at the T.T. Races held in 1936 on the Ards Circuit. Nowadays my family turn up their noses at ox tongue. The wheel is now turning full circle as everything on the farm in those days was organically produced with animals given no supplements and crops no chemicals.

If I had the authority and the where-with all to bring it about one lady from Straid should have been awarded the Membership of the British Empire for her devotion over and above
the call of duty of her calling which was that of post woman.

Annie Moore (nee') Cameron's mother carried the mail from Straid Post Office for many years and handed the job over to Annie in about 1943 and for the next quarter of a century was a faithful worker for both the Post Office and the countryside in general.

Annie covered around 20 miles a day on foot and when one tends to remember that in those days, there were no post codes and the roads were named by the occupiers upon them.

There was another draw back which Annie had to take in her stride and this perhaps why she had more knowledge about the families of the district than any living person in those days of no computers.

It has been explained elsewhere in this volume how our forefathers came from the Scottish borders and Galloway to occupy the lands left derelict by the final occupation of Ulster by the troops of Queen Elizabeth I after the Flight of the Earls in 1607.

As happened in the eighteenth century with the emigrants from the New World writing home and inviting relations out to a better life so did our settlers send for Scottish relations and many families of the same name encamped in the same town land. The only way to differentiate between these people was to give them a nickname as a method of distinguishing each family. The family name of Kennedy is synoptic of this with different men and to distinguish the same forename Sam's Robert given the forename of Red Ned, Quiet Robert or maybe a number of Sam's lived in the Irish Hill district where all the Kennedy's seemed to settle and were called Jock's Sam or Carpenter Sam.

Thus Annie had to know each person intimately and her expertise in this field was very evident when her successor followed on.

One of Annie's worst experiences was during the winter of 1962/63 when a blizzard caught her at about 800 feet above sea level at Ardboley. She recounts that the first day of snow was the worst and during the next fortnight farmers helped her considerably by cutting lanes and roads. The difference between the heavy snow in 1963 and that in 1937 and 1947 was the fact that farm machinery was becoming more sophisticated with hydraulic frontloading shovels to clear snow or bulldoze it to the side.

The local Orange men belonging to Straid L.O.L. 502 never appreciated how much work Annie put in on their behalf. Her husband Robert, also known as Bobbie, held the post of Secretary of the Lodge for many years and at any time when hospitality was needed Annie acted as a one woman committee and supplied all that was required.

The author was delighted when Straid Royal Black Preceptory No.22 honoured Annie by asking her to unfurl their new banner a number of years ago. May Annie live long in Straid to enjoy her well-earned retirement.

The author heard a remarkable story not long ago concerning a well-respected family in the area today. A boy in Co Tyrone called Jack Kerr was born circa 1764 but both parents died when he was nine years old and whether he had neither kith or kin or was being abused he left Co Tyrone and walked all the way eventually finding himself in Straid.

How he fed himself and finished up in Straid is a mystery but he finished up at that age working in Hutchinson's of Seskin Road in the flourishing scutch and corn mill and the splendid farm there at that time. As the years went on he married a Rebecca Kennedy, presumably from the Irish Hill, and had one son who was a stone mason and who built Straidlands for the Crymble family and who had a son born in 1821 who followed his father's footsteps in becoming a stone mason and who helped to build Garron Tower for Lady Londonderry before the famine.

When this man was forty-nine he built Straid Orange Hall and the author has been told that before the cut stones on the walls were pointed with cement every stone could be seen to be perfectly cut and fitting perfectly with its neighbour. Anyone looking at this stonework could not help but admire an art that has now sadly passed. One of this stone mason's daughters married a man called Boyd the latest men of that family being known as Boyd's the Painters, men of outstanding ability in the painting and decorating world whose expertise was much in demand. These painters father had a brother called John Kerr Boyd, keeping the old name of Kerr in the family but in Staid was inevitably known as John Carr Boyd and was one of the best shots with a .22 rifle that author has ever seen. Johnny worked in the Green Bleach Works in Ballyclare but when not working could be seen scouring the country looking to kill foxes. In those days nearly all Churches ran Bazaars and Flower Shows and had shooting galleries for .22 rifles but poor Johnny Carr was barred from usage of same as at one time or another he had scooped all the prizes. He would now days be a sensation at Bisley.

Not long ago the author heard Julie Andrews in "The Sound of Music" singing "These are a few of my favourite things" and one of his favourite things was long ago walking into a byre with about ten cows at night lying comfortably in the heat chewing the cud and grunting with satisfaction.

When he looks today at cows lying on slats over a tank of cow dung eating a cold collage of silage and water and filthy with their own excreta he wonders if these cows would not produce more milk in more comfortable conditions. He has heard that cattle produce a lot of methane gas thus increasing the hole in the ozone layer but he fears little gas is produced in silos and the ozone layer has already been damaged by the aforementioned cows in the byre lying farting with contentment.

Conversely I had a few things in the farming calendar, which I detested, with all my being. I would think that no farmer under the age of thirty would ever have seen a marrow-stem kale. The plant was sown widely years ago usually where potato fields drills rant into points with each drill getting shorter. This plant grew about five feet tall and about nine inches in circumference with the marrow inside the stem being extremely succulent to cattle. It resembled, when growing, a huge Brussel sprout without the sprouts but with very large leaves. Imagine if you will, cutting this plant at the base with a billhook and the resulting shower of water leaving one soaking. Thinning turnips around the 12th July was another chore he detested while pulling same in winter and "snedding" them, (removing the soil from the roots) was a heartbreaking job in frosty weather. Having given my pet hates in those days I would not have missed them for anything and only feel a great deal of nostalgia for a portion of my life and time which nevermore shall return.

A place which now has been forgotten about in Straid was a clachan of small houses lying between Dairylands Road and Ballylagan Road. This area was known as the "Cunney Wharry" but was officially termed "Coney Warren on the map due to the pre-ponderance of rabbits in the vicinity. The inhabitants of these houses worked either in Wilson's corn mill on the Ballylagan Road or in Hutchinson's corn and scrutch mill on the Seskin Road.

It must be remembered that these corn mills did much more than grind corn, as flour came from grinding wheat and kiln dried corn was made into oatmeal. Now a days the young do not know where their food comes from nor do they know how it is produced.

In conclusion the author feels it is incumbent upon him to put into perspective the relevant change in the financial position of the agricultural community as opposed to urban workers who can rely on, at least, an annual rise in salary commensurate with inflation.

In the early 1950's hen eggs were selling ex farm for 3/6 per dozen (17_pence) now and a gallon of petrol retailed at 4 shillings (20 pence) while today the author buys Curry's excellent eggs at £1.00 per dozen in Jackson's of Ballynure, but his diesel now costs £5.00 per gallon.

He feels that the general public were put at a severe disadvantage when the good old English pound tumbled from 240 pence to 100 pence.

It is his eternal hope that agricultural produce will receive, in the future, the financial rewards it deserves and reimburse the agriculturist who has to battle with weather, government and the European commission.

An 'Age Old Scene' one hopes will never change.

Straid Farmers' Union

The Farmers' Union Branches in many districts met in the local school, with the "Master" acting as secretary. The subscription rate in the fifties was six pence per pound of the Poor Law Valuation of ones farm but small attendances at many Branch meetings and the big increase in ownership of cars in the farming community led to the holding of joint meetings of several branches in central locations. Twelve branches in North West Londonderry agreed to form a group and due to its success grouping of branches in other areas with full time Group secretaries to organise meetings, collect the Union membership subscriptions, to be agents for the National Farmers Union Mutual Insurance Society, an Insurance Company where paid up members of the Union received discount when paying.

This fundamental change resulted in the loss of individual small branches and their Secretaries who were compensated by the Mutual Society for their loss of revenue as agents.

Groups were formed gradually and the whole reorganisation was only completed in 1979.

Some branches continued to operate within the Group and in other areas the Group meeting have taken the place of Branch meetings.

Each Group had at first one Group Secretary but increase in insurance business mainly due to the increase of tractors and self propelled vehicles, led to the appointment of Joint and Junior Group Secretaries and in 1988 there were fifty-nine Group Secretaries with in each of the twenty-four Groups in Northern Ireland.

Although there are now no individual branches of the Farmers' Union in various villages as they now operate in the districts with Straid in S.E. Antrim District, at one time, especially in the 1930's, Straid had a very active Branch. They met in the old school house which in the 1923 Education Act had been changed from the National School to Public Elementary School although the old National School plaque still was displayed above the door.

The School had two rooms divided from each other by a sliding partition and on a night when the Farmers' Union had its Annual General Meeting and concert this partition was folded back and the two rooms were usually packed with farmers and their families. Once the business of the A.G.M. was over tea and sandwiches were distributed, afterwards a social evening was enjoyed by all.

It must be remembered by all that in a time of no television and very few radios in the 30's everyone had to make each others recreation and in that period just after the birth of Northern Ireland there was a piano in every home and a fiddle hanging up on every wall and many were the local entertainers at every concert.

One entertainer who never missed Straid's night was Rev. R. J McIlmoyle a Covenanting minister from Dervock in Co Antrim. Nowadays these Covenanters are known as The Reformed Presbyterians and Rev. McIlmoyle was no stranger to Straid as he had preached in Ballyclare Church on the Ballycorr Road and lived for four years in number 88 Ballyeaston Road, Ballyclare, which was then the Manse for the Church before he got the call to Dervock.

His Reverence was prominent in the Union from its early days by being a valued member on its Executive and Sheep Committees.

He travelled all over Ulster and was a valued Speaker at all Annual Socials where he possessed a fund of farming and other humorous stories. He also had the reputation of never telling the same joke again in the same venue no matter how many times he attended. He was an expert Border Leister Sheep Judge and ran a flock on the few acres the Church owned in Dervock.

Another entertainer was a local lad called Davy Hunter whose fund of recitations in Ulster Scots was superb. His rendering of a piece called "The tarrin of the coo" always brought the house down followed by a piece called "The bonnie wee winda" where the author remembers the lines "Wae his heed stuck in the winda, the bonnie wee winda, the nicest wee winda that iver ye saw".

It was at this time that many branches organised outings in the summer to places of interest and the author well remembers his first sea journey to the Isle of Man on an old passenger ship called Mona's Isle. One old gentleman kept shouting to come to the other side as everyone was on the side facing the dock and he swore the boat would "coupe"!

The Union had a Stand in the King's Hall at Balmoral until 1959 when it built its own pavilion near the jumping enclosure in which members are provided with a meeting place and Refreshments during the May Show each year.

The Author feels that, as in the 1930's farmers now must be really organised to oppose the enormous power of the big supermarkets who at this moment can dictate the price given to farmers and he thinks the country will rue the day when bottled water costs more than fresh milk.

Prizes at the 1945 show

Straid Young Farmers' Club

The Young Farmers' Clubs came about as a progression to the Ulster farmers' Union, which itself was formed from a public meeting arranged on December 14th 1917 in the Ulster Hall, Belfast. For years there had been farming organisations throughout the country which carried on campaigns for tenant rights, organised Agricultural Shows and Ploughing Matches but this was the first time there was a central organisation of some strength to co-ordinate the various local and sectional interests in negotiations with the Government.

Several branches of the Farmers' Union had formed Junior Members' Clubs and the Executive of the Union recommended in October 1929 that branches of the Unions should encourage the formation of Young Farmers' Clubs.

The Union provided office accommodation for an organiser, R M Kimber, who had been brought over from England to set up the Young Farmers' Clubs. The Union's Education Committee undertook financial responsibility for the administration of a grant from the Carnegie Trust for the first few years of the Clubs' formation. It must be remembered that at this period in the 1930's farm prices were at slump level, money was scarce, especially among young farmers, and it was not until the second world war brought prosperity that we find Clubs opening up in the Forties. In 1937 the Clubs became an independent organisation with offices in the same building as the Farmers' Union. The clubs provided many leaders for the Union in the days that followed.

The Young Farmers' Club were formed at a meeting in January 1930 organised by A W S Armour, Editor of the Northern Whig at that time and supported by the then President of the Ulster Farmers' Union, Humphrey Jamieson. It, to my mind, is a remarkable coincidence that on a blustery March evening in 1941 an event took place in the schoolhouse in Straid which was to have important consequences now in 2007, sixty-six years later. The coincidence was the fact that the schoolmaster organised the event. He was S Windrum Armour, son of the aforementioned, S W Armour organiser of the Young Farmers' Clubs. W.S. was universally, of course, known as "Windy" and he called a meeting in March with this idea of his to form a Club in Straid. From the old headquarters in Belfast, the Y.F.C's. did not share their new headquarters in 18 Donegall Square East with the U.F.U. until 1945 when it was officially opened. A representative of the council called J B Kirkpatrick and Windy pulled the meeting together. J. B. was an eccentric little comedian with amazing organisational skills and a Club wa formed with T Leslie Wilson, President, W James Greer, Club Leader, Sylvia Banford, Hon. Secretary and David Boyd, Treasurer

Straid was one of the last Clubs to be formed because in a Larne Times report of 22nd February 1941 we find a report of a Public Speaking contest at Ballylinney where the winners came from Ballylinney, Gleno, Rathmore and Cairncastle.

Mrs R.H. Wilson and Mrs J. Furnace with little Miss Armour at the show

Gleno Valley Y.F.C. had hosted an Agricultural Show in June 1941 and this acted as a catalyst to Straid to do the same in 1942. Various functions were held to raise money and many firms from the farming community donated silver cups and trophies. Two meal firms in particular spent a lot of money helping Clubs to run functions. E T Green and White, Tompkins and Courage put money in for prizewinners

and White Tompkins and Courage swelled many an agricultural heart by admiring their splendid turnout of two fine Clydesdales pulling a brewer's dray.

Straid's first show was an outstanding success in June 1942 in fields kindly lent for the event by the President Mr T L Wilson. There was an outstanding entry of agricultural animals including sheep and living in a time of 4 x 4's and large trailers it perhaps sobering to think back to those days and remember that farmers within reasonable distance of Straid walked their animals to the Show carrying meal and hay to feed them on arrival as they did not want their stock to have full stomachs when walking as evacuation of their bowels would have spoiled their carefully washed and manicured bodies.

We can now read about dynasties being formed from small beginnings and Straid Show has the distinction of having two.

By word of mouth a request came in front of the Show Committee to permit a Nathaniel Hunter Hanvey of Larne and a William Robert Jenkins (a.k.a. as Billy Rab) of Ballynure for permission to attend the Show and sell fruit from a spring cart.

This was granted and on the sweltering day of the Show their produce on the spring cart was sold within the hour and they forced their long suffering pony to trot to Ballyclare where they purchased all the fruit that the shops in Ballyclare had for sale.

These two gentlemen had permission from all functions run in the agricultural community during the summer and in the winter of 1942 N H Hanvey started to produce teas at various functions.

Prior to the 1943 Show Hunter Hanvey promised 30 free teas on the day if he could have the full catering rights for the Show Dance on the following Friday evening. This was granted and it shows the popularity in those days of the Y.F.C. dances at which there never was any trouble and the strongest beverage besides tea was lemonade that Straid paid for 250 teas at three shillings each (15 pence in today's currency) and charged 5 shillings (25 pence) entry fee leaving a profit of £50.00. Hunter Hanvey obtained the job of supplying all dances in East Antrim and further away and he and his daughters opened a very successful restaurant in Larne's Main Street.

W R Jenkins went on to rear and fatten pigs in little home built buildings in a spare piece of land outside Ballynure belonging to a John McRoberts where he made a fortune in black market pork in Belfast and subsequently purchased a farm on the Templepatrick Road. Both men are now deceased but from those small beginnings it is very edifying to note that Hunter Hanvey's son, Nathaniel is still carrying on the catering part of the business and is a great boon to farmers at the local auction marts.

Straid Y.F.C. went on from there to one success after another. After the resignation of W J Greer as Club Leader after two years when he joined the Ministry of Agriculture, the Club Leader was Samuel Agnew of Ballyeaston, a man of outstanding character and organising skills and a few years older than the rest of us thus ensuring that, at one look from him, we immediately became quiet. From then the Club went on from strength to strength producing "kitchen sink" drama plays through an excellent Dramatic Society directed by Sam.

Just at this time the headquarters of the Young Farmers' Clubs of Ulster started exchange visits with other countries, Hugh McCrone Jun., being the first to visit America, Andrew Boyd, Poland while John and Fiona Ferguson visited Australia.

Straid Y.F.C. was and still is to the forefront in stock judging and public speaking and indeed one of the fondest memories of the author is being awarded the Co Antrim Cup for public speaking in Ballyclare Town Hall for 18-21 years of age and beating John Johnston of Kilraughts Y.F.C. by one point. John went on in after life to become the producer of "Farming Today" on Radio Ulster for many years which Richard Wright produces now on the same programme at 6.30 a.m. Monday to Friday. It will be seen from the accompanying photographs how Straid progressed down the years and in March 2007 they celebrated 65 years of progress but the author disputes this anniversary due to the fact that the Club was founded in 1941 and the fact remains that if it had been founded in March 1942 there is no way a fledgling organisation could have had the time or the money to run the successful Show of 1942 in two months. *Long may they reign.*
(More pictures on page 74).

(L-R): Jim Mc Carley & Irene Shaw,
Mr & Mrs William Beattie at a club function

Straid Women's Institute

It has been a standing joke in the author's household for many years that, due to his membership of so many organisations throughout the years, the only one who would not accept his membership was the Women's Institute!

This wonderful women's organisation, fondly known as the W.I. was formed in Straid Orange Hall on 5th March 1945, and was called together by Mrs John Furniss, the wife of the manager of bauxite mines on Straid Hill up to the end of the First World War.

It must be remembered by those born after the second World War ended in the autumn of 1945 that the countryside had for five years been steeped in stygnian darkness due to a strict black-out with no street lights and every house with heavy curtains to restrict light.

With petrol rationed for years and with the allies winning the Battle of the Atlantic an easing on the fuel front was felt and this, together with the utmost certainty that war was marching to a close, led to a great feeling of relief and thankfulness that the bad days were coming to an end. Coupled with the liberation of the female sex who had proved themselves equal to males with war work, the time was ripe for women to organise.

Thus it was on that March night that a Mrs Frizell who was an Area Organiser for the W.I. took the Chair and proceeded with the election of Office Bearers for the coming year.

The first President was Mrs Furniss and Vice Presidents were Mrs Brooks, wife of the Congregational minister and Mrs McMullen, wife of a Belfast Telegraph photographer, who had taken up residence near Straid on account of the Belfast blitz.

Mrs May Thompson was elected Secretary with Mrs J D Boyd Treasurer. A Committee was formed which was tasked to meet for half an hour in the Orange Hall before the main meeting on the fourth Monday of every month. All the ideas for helping the home economy of that time were explored but only the villagers had electricity as power came in 1938 and went straight to Ballynure but due to the war in 1939 there was no street lighting in any village. The W.I. took on a new life in 1955 when electricity was available to all farms if the owner requested same. Those who took advantage of the offer had to pay what was known a standing charge for many years for a condenser to reduce the power from the main line down to 240 volts.

This period of time was the zenith of the period of learning of local Domestic Economy as it was then called. During the war years there was an organisation called the Ministry of Food who took everything to do with food rationing which was only phased out in 1953.

Well-known then electric manufacturers sent representatives round the halls to demonstrate the advantages of cooking by electricity and produced recipes for trying out at home.

Many ladies cast anxious eyes over their baked produce taken to the local flower shows and Church soirees of that time in competition to see who had the most skilful baking hands.

Those were the days when children in schools aged 10 to 14 years were taught to bake and many a cooking range had to be black-leaded by the pupils. It is a great tribute to the older generations that the delicious sponges, cakes, pastry and shortbread were enjoyed by all. Regrettably now-a-days the art has been lost by the rising generations due to the expansion of fast food outlets and supermarkets.

Straid W.I. today goes on from strength to strength with Mrs. Marion Ferguson President and Chairperson, Miss Jane Ferguson Secretary and the Treasurer Mrs Valerie Green. The organisation in entirety held its 75th birthday in Castle Coole in Co Fermanagh from the 4th – 5th May 2007.

Perhaps no greater tribute could be paid to Straid's contribution to continuity in a rural community by having in May 2007 the grand daughter of the first Secretary of the branch, Miss Judith Thompson, give a display in flower arranging and long may this continue to flourish.

A number of years ago the W.I. Ladies left the Orange Hall as a meeting place because the stairs had become an obstacle to many of the older members and met in the school on the Irish Hill Road and the author can remember speaking to one rather large lady who complained about the chairs being too small for her. This reminded me about the story of the arthritic lady sitting on the hard church pew for one and half hours and telling the minister to cut his sermon down as, in her opinion, her head could only take in what her backside could "thole" (take). One thing the author is eagerly awaiting is Straid emulating its sisters of the W.I. in England bringing out a nude calendar which happened to be a great success but whether or not this comes about or not the populace of Straid and district wish the Women's Institute a long and happy life in the future to continue the bonding of the rural community together in an ever changing world.

I cannot finish writing about the W.I. in Straid without quoting my namesake Sir Walter, who wrote in 1821 concerning women:

> "O Woman! In our hours of ease
>
> Uncertain, coy and hard to please
>
> And variable as the shade.
>
> By the light quivering aspen made:
>
> When pain and anguish wring the brow
>
> A ministering angel thou!

Enough said!!

Straid Masonic Lodge 276

The first Warranted Lodge to sit in the Straid District was 923 and the Warrant was issued on 2nd December 1802 in the names of William Junkin, Malcolm Hutchinson and William Hutchinson and continued under this number until 1824. All the Orders at any time always desire the lowest Warrant number obtainable and Straid had been on search for one and was successful in the quest and on 6th January 1825 were granted Warrant No. 276 in exchange for 923 in the names of David Weatherup, Samuel Weatherup and Samuel McKee.

It is interesting to note that No.276 was first issued on 5th January 1758 to a Lodge sitting in Monastereven, Co Kildare and worked from then until 5th January 1823.

Around the middle of the 19th century times in agriculture were difficult and before the start of the Industrial Revolution in Belfast with the linen mills, shipyards, rope works and many other ancillary industries starting up people living in the country areas with large families on small farms had little disposal income and many masons could not afford the dues required and around 1864 these facts prompted the few remaining Brethren to ask the Grand Lodge to accept the Warrant on trust for a limited period.

It was restored again on 28th October 1865 and it is interesting to note that under Warrant No. 276, 776 members have been registered in Grand Lodge between the years 1825 and 2002 (latest figures)

Until 1896, when the present Masonic Hall was built the Lodge had no permanent home and usually minute books and other matters including equipment was kept in individual hands resulting in much being lost.

This was no worse than individual clergymen keeping records of marriages and deaths as their personal possessions until they were obliged to keep official records in the1840's.

It will be seen in the chapter elsewhere in this book that a mason called James Kerr had built the Orange Hall in 1870 and it is reasonable to suppose that an amount of money would be forwarded to the Orangemen from the Masons to be allowed to sit in it. This is indeed what happened and we find the Masonic Lodge used the Hall from 1871 to 1896.

During this period two rather unsavoury incidents occurred one involving Orangemen. On June 3rd 1893 the Lodge at Labour was interrupted by a mob of non-Masons in the Orange Hall attempting to force open the door and disrupt the meeting. Incensed at this intrusion Brother McAllister seized the Tyler's Sword intent on confronting the mob single-handed but wisdom prevailed and the jewels and other equipment were safely placed in the wooden chest kept for that purpose and the brethren left the Hall untouched by the mob. A communication from Body in August from the Provincial Grand Lodge informed the Straid Lodge No.276 that it intended to recall the Warrant as the Lodge was not working in a building that was dedicated to Masonry, it was, after strong representation and an explanation, allowed to remain in Straid.

In the early days after the building of the Orange Hall the two Orders used same to their mutual advantage with the exception of one or the other holding nights that clashed with other.

This harmony was put to the test when some prominent members of the Orange Lodge sought admission to 276 and were rejected and the relationship between the two bodies worsened until a point was reached where it was found necessary to appoint a Board of Arbitration to sort out the claims of both bodies. The finding of the Board was that the Hall should be divided into two floors with Lodge 276 occupying the lower one and Orange Lodge 502 the upper.

The Orange Lodge members ignored this ruling however and continued with an aggressive attitude towards the Masons until they formed the opinion that the only solution to the problem was to cancel the agreement and subsequently left under an amount agreed by the Arbitrators and Umpire which amounted to £102.10.0.

This was the catalyst, which ignited the desire of the Masons to have a Hall of their own, and a Bazaar was held in Ballyclare at the bottom of the Hillhead Road, which netted the amazing sum of £351 in those days. This took place on the 20th and 21st August 1887 when the British Empire was in its zenith and money was being made by the citizens who had left the country areas for Belfast, the fastest growing city in the Empire in those days.

The present Hall was the built on the Seskin Road and was officially opened by Mrs McCalmont, wife of Colonel McCalmont, M.P. for East Antrim at that time on 4th July 1896.

So the Lodge continued for many years until a Mason called Robert Robinson, after spending 35 years of his life as Principal of Tandragee National School, came to Straid. He, in Tandragee, had founded Tandragee Council of Knight Masons No.35 and was desirous to found same in Straid, which would pioneer this Council in the Six-Mile Water valley.

Eight members from No. 276 travelled to Tandragee and received all the degrees of the branch of the Order and at a specially convened meeting of Council 35, Straid Council of Sir Knights No.44 was born.

It was planned to constitute the Council in February 1947, which month figures in Knight Masonry but any one of the age of the author can remember well the fierce blizzard which struck the country on 22nd January 1947 and lasted for six weeks and the event had to be postponed until early May when Straid Council No. 44 was launched and became one of the success stories of Freemasonry in the Six Mile Valley District.

Long may Masonry flourish in Straid in spite of Government doing its best to stifle anything to do with Masonry or its employees be they police or civil servants.

Picture Gallery of Young Farmer's Club

(L-R): Elizabeth Hill, (Secretary), Mrs J. Park, (President's Wife), Miss Joan Dobbs, President Y.F.C. and our club leader at a function.

Marian Ferguson (Rt Back Row) Cup Winner at Y.F.C. in 1975.

Guests at a Straid Y.F.C. Gala Night many years ago.

Straid Lodge at the Field in the early 1970's

The Loyal Orders
L.O.L. Straid. 502

The Orange Order is the largest Protestant organisation in Northern Ireland with roughly 75,000 members, with others in the Republic of Ireland.

In 1795, a clash between Protestants and Catholics at a place called the Diamond, Loughgall, Co Armagh led to some of those involved to swear a new oath to uphold the Protestant faith and be loyal to the King and his heirs giving birth to the Orange Order.

Since then the Order's principles and aims, and those of similar organisations it is related to, have changed little.

It regards itself as defending civil and religious liberties of Protestants and seeks to uphold the rule and ascendancy of a Protestant monarch in the United Kingdom.

Straid L.O.L. has a claim that very few lodges have. It was issued it's first Warrant, which was a military one No.502, and was issued to a Colonel Buckley in 1798. This date is significant in that it was the date of the United Irishmen uprising and Colonel Buckley was Commanding Officer of the North Hampton Fencibles and the author suspects he took as allies a group of citizens who were against the Rising, as many of the loyal Volunteers were Orangemen and used to augment the British Army as the Ulster Defence Regiment were used until their disbandment.

This in effect brought the United Irishmen's Rising to the brink of civil war where perhaps three sons and their father were rebels while a fourth son was an Orangeman and a Volunteer.

Warrant 502 then lay dormant until it was re-issued to Straid in Larne District No.1 in 1856 and renewed in 1876 after the Hall was opened in 1870.

It now seems incredible to us in the year of our Lord 2007 that Straid L.O.L. probably sat during the American Civil War where 600,000 lives were lost in the abolition of Slavery although the British Empire had abolished same in 1833 due to the eminent politician and evangelical social reformer Wilbert Wilberforce.

The author joined the Order in Straid in 1947, the year of the biggest fall of snow to hit East Antrim ever, at a time when there was around sixty paid up members with around forty attending the meetings and on the evening of the January meeting, which was the installation of Officers for the ensuing year, over 100 people sat down to what was then known as a meat tea supplied by a Mrs Thompson and helpers from Carrickfergus.

The Secretary at this time was a Bob Semple and the post of Worshipful Master alternated between a few of the older members. A stalwart called David Robinson was for over 20 years Treasurer and when numbers started to flag David, in my opinion, paid the rates and paid for coal for the open fire.

A William Gamble in the eighteen and nineteen hundreds held sway in the Lodge as Worshipful Master for well over twenty years but depriving ordinary Members from being elevated to the Chair and the Deputy Chair.

After a number of years the aforementioned Bob Semple resigned as Secretary owing to a change in employment and Robert Moore stepped in and continued for many years. When Bob, as he was universally known to all, stepped down due to failing health, the author held the position for many years under a variety of good Worshipful Masters until 2004, when, after a very detailed examination of both his conscience and a list of the laws to which the member must adhere, there is one which the Orangeman should resist the ascendancy of the Roman Catholic Church but always abstaining from all uncharitable words, actions or sentiments towards his Roman Catholic brethren – he resigned.

This sadly has disappeared owing to the presence of Sinn Fein and its underhand machinations of promoting these concerned residents Associations to oppose Orange Marches where they have taken place for many years but the population has changed.

It saddened him to see brethren in regalia stoning the forces of law and order on television but worse was to come when, after being prosecuted in the Courts the same brethren were allowed to stay in their respective Lodges. Images on television of protestors blocking the traffic while brandishing Orange regalia with loyalist paramilitary figures in the background sickened him and led to his resignation. He has not regretted this decision and feels the urban Brethren are falling into traps set purposely and when the late Harold Gracey, Portadown District W.M. would not publicly condemn violence linked to the protests this was the straw that broke the camel's back.

For those who are not in the Loyal Orders a look at the history and working of the same will not come amiss.

A Black Banner unfurling in Straid, showing a younger author and his wife -1960's

Royal Black Preceptory 22

The Royal Black Institution, also known as the Royal Black Preceptory or the Imperial Grand Black Chapter of the British Commonwealth is a Protestant fraternal society.

It was formed in 1797, two years after the formation of the Orange Order. The Society is formed from Orangemen and although separate organisations is often referred to as the senior of the Loyal Orders.

Its headquarters are in Lurgan and members refer to each other as "Sir Knight" whereas in the Orange Order the members are referred to as Brother or Brethren. Its basis is the promotion of the Scriptures and the principle of the Protestant Reformation.

The major parade of the year is held on the last Saturday in August, except Fermanagh, who holds their earlier. A very colourful annual parade is also held in Scarva, Co. Down on 13th July and can have up to 100,000 spectators attending what is commonly known as "The Sham Fight".

It appears to the author, having belonged to both organisations for over 50 years, that the Royal Black Institution has adopted a more conciliatory attitude to the more contentious parades than the Orange Order and it is his mind that its parades are less sensitive in several areas where the population is mixed half and half religiously due to the absence of what is known as "Kick the Pope Bands" and the rabble rousing followers of such bands.

The Preceptory reflects the more middle class, rural, respecta ble elite elements of Orangeism. Certain critics see it as being ritualistic in a similar way to Freemasonry.

There are eleven initiatory degrees with a final retrospective overview degree.

Straid R.B.P. and Straid Orange Order have for the past number of years had two members without whose expertise in keeping buildings in good order, the Orange Hall and car park would not be in the splendid shape it is today. The late Fred McLean and Samuel Armstrong have kept the premises in first class order due to Fred's expertise in Carpentry and Sam's in interior decorating, but die to Fred's passing and Sam's increasing years a void will be found in the upkeep of the premises.

The numbers in Straid Black Preceptory increased dramatically when Ballynure L.O.L. came and joined en masse but I fear that T.V. and other organisations have had a deteriorating effect on old institutions but the author wishes them all many happy years to come.

The north east entrance to the mines

The Bauxite Mines

Bauxite is a naturally occurring aluminium oxide $Al_0\_nH_0$, the commercial source of Aluminium consisting of various proportions of the trihydrated and the monohydrated forms.

There used to be deposits of ore all over Co Antrim, usually found near deposits of salt. It used to be mined on the Irish Hill and before that on the Fair Hill, Ballynure where a small deposit ran out leaving Straid to produce ore up until the end of the Great War and closed in 1923.

A gentleman called George G Blackwell, a native of Liverpool, formed a company with an Alexander Sunderland from Larne called Bauxite Co., Irwell Chambers, Fazaherley, Liverpool and upon determining that Alum Clay was in abundance under the hill above Straid in 1875, started to mine.

For 43 years Alum Clay was mined and shipped to Larne via Ballymena and Larne Railway Companies' narrow gauge railway which had only opened in 1874, but that meant the ore had to be transported to Ballynure Station on what is now known as Church Road.

When enough ore was landed at Ballynure, labourers were sent to load the ore to go to Antrim Iron Ore Co at what is now called Redlands, the ground coloured red due to the ore at Larne Harbour. The author has in his possession a copy of a contract between Sir Hugh Smylie and his two sons and the Antrim Iron Ore Co to ship ore from Larne and Glenarm for 3 pence per ton – no wonder Sir Hugh and family were very comfortable in the Drumalis buildings in Larne.

The Straid mines manager was an Englishman, John Furniss, 38 years of age in 1901 whose wife and elder son James were also English but three other sons, John, George and Hubert were born in Straid. John was universally known as Jack, to distinguish him from his father.

Jack was the Furniss best known around Straid after returning from Boarding School in 1911 and becoming a trainee mine manager. Politics, as usual, was the main topic of the day due to P.M.Gladstone's Home Rule Bill. Jack, being educated, was a must as an Officer in the Ulster Volunteer Force at that time.

On one famous night of 24th April 1914, about which much has been written and has gone down in history books as the Larne gun running. Jack Furniss, being 23 years of age and an Officer in the U.V.F. played a pivotal part in this affair which is very much part of our history.

Into the bowels of Straid Hill went 300 Mauser rifles and 6000 rounds of .300 inch ammunition, 20 rounds per rifle. These were distributed around an area to Volunteers from Carnmoney to Larne. Many of these rifles were on farms in the author's youth but could not be used, as .300 ammunition could not be got as the British Army used .303 sizes in its famous Lee Enfield rifles.

Many of these Mausers were hurriedly dumped in lakes or buried when the Army started to search the countryside for illicit arms in the early seventies.

In 1914 war was declared on Germany and the men of the U.V.F. volunteered under Lord Carson to fight for King and Country in the now famous battles of World War I, the most important being the Battle of the Somme where the Ulstermen attached to 36th Ulster Division, excelled themselves but fell in thousands, 5600 casualties on 1st July 1916 alone! Jack Furniss had the distinction of being the first Officer in the 108th Brigade to which the 36th belonged, to be awarded the Military Cross. He joined the Civil Service when the mines closed down and lived in Derriaghy near Lisburn, from where he was buried in January 1957 aged 67 years.

The author remembers talking to a Straid man, David Montgomery, born in 1885 who was foreman in the mines when they closed. At that time the Antrim Iron Ore Co., had a mine working in Ballintoy and Davy got the chance of a foreman's job there. Being 38years of age and very fit he rode a bicycle on a Monday morning to Ballintoy and returned on Saturday afternoon a distance in those days on worse roads than now of 65 miles.

About Straid mine he told me that two entrances were used, one to the North East side of the hill where the ore was fairly near the surface and another was directly South West but entered by a shaft its depth variable from 90 to 150 feet.

It must be remembered that at the end of the twentieth century nearly all the work was don e manually and one can imagine the toil in picking, breaking and shovelling one ton of ore into the bogies which ran to the bottom of the two hills called the Dippa. This ore had then to be transferred to farm carts by shovel and then taken to Ballynure. Two men, father and son, called McBride were on the mines books as "tree-ers" and the author has always thought that a tree-er was a horseman who towed a second horse in a cart as no animal on its own could pull a ton plus the weight of the cart up the Dippa brae.

The word "tree" was a term used in the days of the horse for using an iron or wooden shaft about three foot long with hooks at each end and a coupling in the middle, the hooks being attached to horses chains or traces as they were called. There were "single trees " and "double trees" for one horse or in a pair and in using what was known as a "trace" horse this single tree would be used. Four carters were used and employed by the firm but outside help was obtained from local farmers when needed at 2s.6p. ($12^1/2$ p now) per ton from the Dippa to Ballynure Narrow Gauge Station.

When the mines closed circa.1923 nothing was done until 1935 when Larne District Council put in pump valves and connected ice cold water from the mines to them and so good is that water, although is now attached to the mains supply, that a firm is bottling Antrim Hills water from the same source.

When the mines closed Straid reverted to its calm rural existence where the workers elsewhere left in the morning and returned in the evening to an undisturbed community.

A pump valve in
Straid village

*This re-constructed farm cottgae was the venue for the last visit of the Society this year,
when the members were entertained and refreshments given by the generosity of the
owner Mr David Bates, a valued member.*

The Newest Organisation

Straid Cultural Heritage and Historical Group was formed in January 2002
with the intention of bringing people together who might have an interest in
the social history of the area. Its initial aim was to record stories of the past be
they factual or folklore.

In 2002, the year of the Queen's Golden Jubilee, a publication called "Straid,
A Glance Back" was produced. Much material was found by the pupils of the
Primary School and in so doing they participated in a Competition run by
Newtownabbey Borough Council in honour of the Jubilee.

The Society have visited other Groups and they in turn have come to Straid
while the winter months have been enjoyed by various speakers coming and
spreading their expertise from knowledge of the now defunct narrow gauge
railway to an excellent talk by a cartographer on local maps.

The meetings are held in the canteen of the Primary School and a much-
enjoyed cup of tea is always available after the meeting.

The author was highly honoured in 2003 when he was elected President of the Group and is very pleased by the way the Office-bearers perform and at present John Jenkins, Chairman, with secretaries Cis Weatherup and Marnie Douglas backing him, he sees no reason to doubt that going from strength to strength is inevitable in an ever rapidly changing world.

Potato harvesting '2007 style'

Finale

The author in his foreword of this book wrote with a heavy heart due to the death of his good friend Archie Reid, that eminent local historian from Ballyclare, now finds at the end he is still of the same frame of mind.

Upon opening the Belfast Telegraph in the middle of July 2007 and seeing the advertisement for planning applications he immediately spotted one for permission to demolish the house and outhouses at No.2 Main Street, Straid to build 14 apartments.

This beautiful Georgian house, adjoining shop and outbuildings, has been the hub around which Straid and its wide environs have existed for over five generations under the name of Thomas Wilson and Sons.

It has been written elsewhere in this book about the continuity of life in rural areas and the writer's father knew four generations of the Wilson family whereas the writer himself remembers Robert Henry Wilson, his son Thomas Leslie and Leslie's son David, all in the shop which supplied all the needs of an agricultural community including all the coal and slack for the village. This trade is now carried on by Messrs. R. J. Blair.

Now this is all gone including the busy Post Office and now we are to have fourteen apartment in its place.

If these apartments are an eyesore or a blot on the landscape when I have left this moral coil and if I am lucky enough to be able to descend with the aid of a pair of golden wings from the Pearly Gates or conversely have to battle my way out from the crowd around the fire down below I shall sit as a nemeses on the shoulder of the Architet and also make the Developer very unhappy.

A 'Horse Hay Rake' draws the hay into rows, which the tumbling paddy then gathers.

A 'Tumbling Paddy'. Known officially as a hay collector but colloqually as 'a Tumbling Paddy', gathers hay behind the horse untill full when it is then tipped over the hay to compress it.

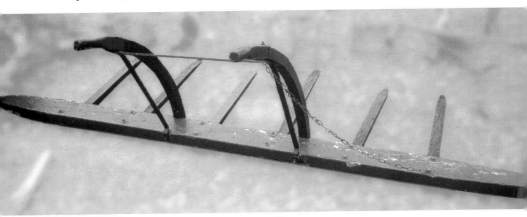

A typical tractor used nowadays on the farm.

This is a 'Benchmark', colloqually known as the 'Crows Foot', on the corner stone of Straid Church and marked on the O.S. maps as 525 feet above sea level.

Towards Ballyboley Hill

Straid Dam, built in 1824 for the Ballynure Cotton Mill, from Bryantang townland.

An enjoyable teabreak among the corn during harvest.